Cordon Bleu

Sauces and Seasonings

Cordon Bleu

Sauces and
Seasonings

CBC / B.P.C. Publishing Ltd.

Published by
B.P.C. Publishing Ltd.,
P.O. Box 20,
Abingdon, Oxon.

Designed by Melvyn Kyte
Printed and bound in England
by Waterlow (Dunstable) Limited

These recipes have been adapted from the Cordon Bleu Cookery Course
published by Purnell in association with the London Cordon Bleu
Cookery School
Principal : Rosemary Hume ; Co-Principal : Muriel Downes
Spoon measures are level unless otherwise stated.

Contents

Introduction

The term 'sauce' covers an infinite variety of culinary tricks for enhancing basic foods. Often a sauce will not only improve the flavour of a dish but make it more digestible, too. And every cook can improvise to give his or her foods an inimitable distinction.

The word is an old French one originally deriving from the Latin 'salsus' which meant salted. This came about from the old habit of preserving meat in salt; the meat would give off a salty liquid which was then mixed with wine, vinegar, honey or sugar and lots of herbs or spices to make a sauce to disguise the flavour of meat that was, to put it politely, no longer at its freshest.

Nowadays we're more subtle about the whole thing. We would no longer dream of serving tainted meat or fish, so we don't need the highly spiced sauces that go with it; instead we go for more delicate flavours that simply improve the natural taste and appearance of the food. There are some long tried favourites, though, that have stood the test of time on sheer dietary merit. Apple sauce with roast pork and mint sauce with lamb are just two of these, where the sauces stimulate the gastric juices which help to digest the rich meats.

When we were choosing the recipes for this book we decided it was impossible to talk about sauces without including some of the foods that go with them, so in many cases we have given the recipes for whole dishes, both savoury and sweet. With others it was possible to say simply 'serve this one with poultry', 'serve this one with fish' and so on. Stuffings are another way of varying the flavours of basic foods and of course it would be impossible to make either sauces or stuffings without seasonings, herbs and spices. Here too we include recipes with examples of their use.

At the end of this book is our usual appendix including notes and basic recipes for items that recur throughout. Also there is a glossary of cooking terms that may not be familiar

7

to everybody. Many experienced cooks will never need to look at the appendix, but if there is something you do not understand you will probably find it explained there.

Making sauces is one of the most exciting kinds of cookery; simple variations can create great gastronomic changes from one basic food. It also allows scope for both the classic cook and the one who likes to experiment. We hope in this book we have provided material for both, for we have included the basic classic sauces and many, many variations.

Rosemary Hume
Muriel Downes

Basic sauces

A clever sauce can transform a simple dish into something superlative. From the basic 'mother' (mère) sauces — white, béchamel, velouté or demi-glace — you can make an infinite variety. Those sauces in this section that are not true mother sauces are never the less useful bases from which variations can be made.

There is no mystique about sauce-making; it's just very important to measure the ingredients exactly because, if the proportion of flour to liquid is wrong, no amount of cooking will give you the right consistency. You can vary the consistency of a white sauce, according to what you are going to use it for, by varying the amount of flour to liquid. But before you start, remember the following points:

1 Weight of fat should be slightly⁴ more than that of flour to give a soft, semi-liquid roux.
2 If the roux is hot, liquid should be warm or cold ; if roux is cold, liquid must be warm. This makes blending easier and avoids a granular texture.

3 Fats used may be butter, margarine, dripping or oil, according to the type of sauce being made.

To make a flowing sauce, to serve as an accompaniment in a separate sauce boat, use $\frac{1}{2}$ oz butter and just under $\frac{1}{2}$ oz flour to $\frac{1}{2}$ pint liquid. For a coating consistency, to coat fillets of fish, eggs or vegetables in the dish in which they are to be served, use $\frac{3}{4}$ oz butter and just under $\frac{3}{4}$ oz flour to $\frac{1}{2}$ pint liquid. For a panade, which is a thick sauce used as a base for binding croquettes, fish or meat creams, use $1\frac{1}{2}$-2 oz butter and just under the same amount of flour to $\frac{1}{2}$ pint liquid.

A brown sauce for everyday use can be made from household stock or even a bouillon cube, and is suitable for serving with cutlets, rissoles and similar dishes. But a true brown 'sauce mère' is in the category of advanced cookery. This is called a demi-glace (half-glaze) and a number of other advanced sauces can be made from it.

For a perfect demi-glace every detail must be right and as this does take time and trouble it is sensible to double or treble the quantities and store the extra in a covered container in the refrigerator, where it will keep for a week. Much of the quality of a demi-glace depends on the stock with which it is made. This should be a clear brown bone stock, free of grease and set to a light, but not too firm, jelly. This will give a good flavour and a fine glossy texture to the sauce. The 'half-glaze' is achieved by the reduction of the bone stock in the sauce. Do not add more flour than the recipe states ; the finished consistency should be that of single cream.

Liaisons

Liaisons play an important part in the making of sauces. The word means a binding together and is a term given to certain ingredients which are used to thicken sauces and soups. A liaison may be a roux, kneaded butter, slaked fécule, or a mixture of egg yolks and cream.

1 Roux is a fat and flour liaison and the weight of fat is slightlly more than that of flour. A roux is the basis of all flour sauces and may be white, blond or brown. To make a white roux, use butter and melt it slowly in a thick pan ; remove from the heat and stir in the flour. To complete the basic sauce, pour on the liquid at once, return to gentle heat and stir until it thickens ; season, bring to the boil and cook for 1 minute. For a blond roux, make with butter as for a white roux, but cook the flour for a few seconds until it is a pale straw colour before adding the liquid. For a brown roux, use dripping or oil and cook the flour slowly to a good russet brown before adding the stock.

2 Kneaded butter (beurre manié) is a liaison mixture of butter and flour in the proportions of almost twice as much butter to flour, worked together on a plate with a fork to make a paste. It is added in small pieces to thicken liquid in which food has been cooked, eg. fish stews and casserole dishes. This is useful when the quantity of liquid remaining in a dish is unknown, making it difficult to know how much flour alone to use for thickening.

Kneaded butter should be added to hot (but not boiling) liquids. Shake pan gently and when the butter has dissolved (indicating flour has been absorbed in liquid) reboil. If the liquid is still not thick enough, the process can be repeated.

3 Fécule, ie. arrowroot or potato flour, should be slaked (mixed) with water or milk and stirred into the nearly boiling liquid off the heat. Once added, reboil and draw aside. Used for ragoûts and casseroles as well as brown sauces.

4 Egg yolks and cream. This mixture may be used to thicken and enrich velouté sauces and some cream soups. The yolk or yolks are worked well together with the cream ; 2-3 tablespoons of sauce are blended into the mixture, a little at a time, and when well blended, the whole is returned to the main bulk of the sauce and stirred in gradually. Reheat, stirring continually, but do not boil. This will cook the egg yolks slowly and so give a particulary creamy consistency to the sauce.

White sauce

$\frac{3}{4}$ oz butter
scant $\frac{3}{4}$ oz plain flour
$\frac{1}{2}$ pint milk
salt and pepper

A white sauce is quick and easy, made in exactly the same way and with same proportions as béchamel, but the milk is not flavoured. It can be used as the base for cheese, onion or other sauces with pronounced flavour, but béchamel is better for mushroom and egg sauces.

Method
Melt the butter in a small pan, remove from heat and stir in the flour. Blend in half the milk, then stir in the rest. Stir this over moderate heat until boiling, then boil gently for 1-2 minutes. Season to taste.

Velouté sauce

$\frac{3}{4}$ oz butter
scant $\frac{3}{4}$ oz plain flour
$\frac{1}{3}$-$\frac{1}{2}$ pint stock
$2\frac{1}{2}$ fl oz top of milk
salt and pepper
squeeze of lemon juice

This sauce is made with a blond roux, at which point liquid is added. This is well-flavoured stock (made from veal, chicken or fish bones, according to dish with which sauce is being served), or liquid in which food was simmered or poached.

Velouté sauces are a base for others, such as caper, mustard, parsley, poulette or suprême.

Method
Melt butter in a saucepan, stir in flour and cook for about 5 seconds (blond roux). When roux is colour of pale straw, draw pan aside and cool slightly before pouring on stock.

Blend, return to heat and stir until thick. Add top of milk, season and bring to boil. Cook 4-5 minutes when sauce should be a syrupy consistency.

Béchamel sauce

Short method

¾ pint milk
slice of onion
6 peppercorns
1 blade of mace
1 bayleaf
1 tablespoon cream
  (optional)

For roux
1 oz butter
scant 1 oz plain flour
salt and pepper

Made on a white roux with flavoured milk added, béchamel can be used as a base for mornay (cheese), soubise (onion), mushroom or egg sauces. Proportions of ingredients may vary in these derivative sauces according to consistency required.

Method
Infuse milk with onion and spices in a covered pan over a low heat for 5-7 minutes, but do not boil. Pour the milk into a basin and wipe the pan out.

To make the roux : melt the butter slowly, remove pan from heat and stir in the flour. Pour on at least one-third of the milk through a strainer and blend together with a wooden spoon. Then add the rest of the milk, season lightly, return to heat and stir until boiling. Boil for not more than 2 minutes, then taste for seasoning. The sauce may be finished with 1 tablespoon of cream.

Long method

For mirepoix
1 small onion
1 small carrot
½ stick of celery
1 oz butter

For roux
1 oz butter
scant 1 oz plain flour
1 pint milk
1 bouquet garni
salt and pepper
pinch of grated nutmeg
1 tablespoon cream
  (optional)

Method
Dice the vegetables finely, and melt 1 oz butter in a large thick pan. Add the vegetables to the pan and press a piece of buttered paper down on top. Cover and cook gently for 8-10 minutes ; do not allow to colour. Turn the mirepoix on to a plate.

Make the roux in the same pan, add one third of milk and set aside. Scald remaining milk (by bringing quickly to the boil and removing from heat immediately) and pour on to the roux, whisking well. Add bouquet garni, seasoning and a little nutmeg.

Stir sauce over heat until it boils, then add mirepoix. Simmer in half-covered pan on low heat for 40 minutes, stirring from time to time. Then run the resulting sauce through a conical strainer, pressing lightly to remove juice. Return to a clean pan for reheating. Add the cream if wished.

Hollandaise sauce

4 tablespoons white wine vinegar
6 peppercorns
1 blade of mace
1 slice of onion
1 small bayleaf
3 egg yolks
5 oz unsalted butter
salt and pepper
1-2 tablespoons single cream, or
  top of milk (optional)
squeeze of lemon juice (optional)

This sauce is sometimes used with another sauce, or is served alone with salmon and fish dishes, and vegetables, eg. broccoli.

Method
Put the vinegar into a small pan with the spices, onion and bayleaf. Boil this until reduced to a scant tablespoon, then set aside.

Cream egg yolks in a bowl with a good $\frac{1}{2}$ oz butter and a pinch of salt. Strain on the vinegar mixture, set the bowl on a pan of boiling water, turn off heat and add remaining butter in small pieces, stirring vigorously all the time.

Watchpoint When adding butter, it should be slightly soft, not straight from refrigerator.

When all the butter has been added and the sauce is thick, taste for seasoning and add the cream or milk and lemon juice. The sauce should be pleasantly sharp yet bland, and should have the consistency of thick cream.

Note : if using hollandaise in another sauce, or making it to keep, omit the cream.

Sauce blanche au beurre

2 oz butter
scant $\frac{1}{2}$ oz plain flour
$\frac{1}{2}$ pint water (boiling)
salt and pepper
good squeeze of lemon juice

Method
Melt a good oz of butter in a pan, stir in the flour off the heat and when smooth pour on all the boiling water, stirring or whisking briskly all the time.

Now add remaining butter in small pieces, stirring it well in. Season and add lemon juice.

Watchpoint If the water is really boiling it will cook flour. On no account bring sauce to the boil as this will give it an unpleasant gluey taste.

Basic brown (demi-glace) sauce

3 tablespoons salad oil
1 small onion (finely diced)
1 small carrot (finely diced)
$\frac{1}{2}$ stick of celery (finely diced)
scant $\frac{3}{4}$ oz plain flour
1 teaspoon tomato purée
1 tablespoon mushroom peelings,
   or 1 mushroom (chopped)
1 pint well-flavoured brown stock
bouquet garni
salt and pepper

Method
Heat a saucepan, put in the oil
and then add diced vegetables
(of which there should be no
more than 3 tablespoons in all).
Lower heat and cook gently
until vegetables are on point of
changing colour; an indication
of this is when they shrink
slightly.

Mix in the flour and brown
it slowly, stirring occasionally
with a metal spoon and scraping
the flour well from the bottom
of the pan. When it is a good
colour draw pan aside, cool a
little, add tomato purée and

chopped peelings or mush-
room, $\frac{3}{4}$ pint of cold stock,
bouquet garni and seasoning.

Bring to the boil, partially
cover pan and cook gently for
about 35-40 minutes. Skim
off any scum which rises
to the surface during this time.
Add half the reserved stock,
bring again to boil and skim.
Simmer for 5 minutes. Add rest
of stock, boil up and skim again.
Watchpoint Addition of cold
stock accelerates rising of scum
and so helps to clear the sauce.

Cook for a further 5 minutes,
then strain, pressing vegetables
gently to extract the juice. Rinse
out the pan and return sauce to
it. Partially cover and continue
to cook gently until syrupy in
consistency. It is now ready to
be used on its own or as a base
for other sauces.

When serving a grill, 1-2
teaspoons of this sauce, added
to a gravy or mixed with the
juices in the grill pan, make a
great improvement.

Sauces for fish

A lightly flavoured, creamy sauce to bring out the subtleties of a delicate white fish, or a sharp, spicy sauce to chase the richness of herrings or mackerel - you will find both in this section.
Before you start to read about sauces for fish, be sure to take note of the basic instructions for making sauces on pages 9 and 10. You may also want to take the basic sauces alone to make a simple fish dish. Whichever way you look at it, a whole range of delicious fish cookery is open to you. And don't forget the possibility of marinating, which is covered on pages 127-131; you may want to make your sauce with the spicy marinating juices.

Suprême sauce

1 oz butter
¾ oz plain flour
½ pint strong fish, or chicken,
   or veal, stock

For liaison
2-3 egg yolks
¼ pint single cream

Method
Make up as for velouté sauce.
   For liaison, work the egg
yolks and cream together
and add about 1 tablespoon of
hot sauce. Add the liaison very
slowly to sauce then reheat
very carefully, without boiling.

Caper sauce 1

1 rounded tablespoon capers
1 dessertspoon parsley (chopped)
½ pint velouté sauce

Serve with white fish, boiled
mutton or rabbit.

Method
Make velouté sauce. Then stir
in the capers and parsley.

Caper sauce 2

½ pint sauce blanche au beurre
2 tablespoons capers (lightly
   chopped)
1 dessertspoon chopped parsley
1 egg yolk (optional)

Method
Make sauce blanche au beurre
and add lightly chopped capers
and chopped parsley to the
completed sauce.
   Caper sauce can have an egg
yolk added, if wished.

Mustard sauce 1

1 teaspoon made mustard
   (French, or English)
½ pint velouté sauce

Serve with boiled fish, grilled
herrings and mackerel.

Method
Make velouté sauce. Mix
mustard with 1 tablespoon of
sauce, then stir into sauce.

Mustard sauce 2

1 dessertspoon French, or 1
   teaspoon made English, mustard
½ pint sauce blanche au beurre
1 egg yolk (optional)

Make sauce blanche au beurre
and then add 1 dessertspoon
French or 1 teaspoon made
English mustard per ½ pint sauce.
Add an egg yolk, if wished.

Sauce bâtarde
(mock hollandaise)

Make ½ pint sauce blanche au
beurre and add 1-2 egg yolks
after the boiling water. Then
add the remaining butter, seasoning and lemon juice.

Mornay (cheese) sauce

$\frac{1}{2}$ pint well-seasoned white, or
béchamel, sauce
1-1$\frac{1}{2}$ oz (2-3 rounded tablespoons)
grated cheese
$\frac{1}{2}$ teaspoon made mustard
(French, or English)

This is basically a white or
béchamel sauce to which
cheese has been added. For a
special occasion, use half
Gruyère and half Parmesan
cheese, which gives the very
best result because you get
richness from the Gruyère and
flavour from the Parmesan. For
everyday cooking, a dry Ched-
dar is quite adequate. If using
Gruyère, which thickens sauce,
reduce basic roux to $\frac{1}{2}$ oz each
butter and flour (1 tablespoon).
If too thick, add a little milk.

This sauce is served with
fish, eggs, chicken, vegetables
(eg. cauliflower) and pasta (see
macaroni cheese, page 60).

Method
Make white or béchamel sauce,
remove from heat and gradually
stir in grated cheese. When well
mixed, add mustard. Reheat
but do not boil.

Watchpoint When adding cheese
to a sauce, always stir it in by
degrees to give a good gloss
and a smooth consistency. After
the cheese has been added, do
not boil the sauce again because
it may give mixture a 'chewy'
consistency.

For mornay sauce with sole,
dry fish well ; if water is left
clinging to it, would make sauce
too thin.

*Fillets of sole in a rich mornay sauce
is a classic fish dish*

White wine sauce 1

1 wineglass dry white wine
1 shallot (chopped)
1 blade of mace
3-4 peppercorns
$\frac{1}{2}$ bayleaf
good $\frac{3}{4}$ oz butter
$\frac{1}{2}$ oz plain flour
$\frac{1}{4}$ pint fish stock
4 fl oz milk
1-2 tablespoons cream
salt and pepper
$\frac{1}{4}$ oz butter (to finish)

Serve with fillets of white fish poached in wine and water.

Method
Put the wine, shallot, herbs and seasoning in a pan and simmer until reduced by half. Melt the butter, blend in the flour, pour on the fish stock and strain in the wine. Stir until boiling, add the milk and boil for 2-3 minutes before adding the cream and seasoning. Stir in the butter just before serving.

Egg sauce

$\frac{3}{4}$ pint béchamel sauce (made with $\frac{3}{4}$
  pint flavoured milk, 1 oz butter,
  1 rounded tablespoon flour)
2 eggs (hard-boiled)

Serve egg sauce with poached cod. This sauce can also be served with turbot or halibut, although shrimp or lobster sauce is traditional.

Method
Prepare the béchamel sauce. Coarsely chop eggs and stir into sauce. Adjust seasoning. **Simple oyster, shrimp or lobster sauce** is made in a similar way. Add a small can of these shellfish (drained) instead of egg to above amount of sauce.

Watercress sauce

2 bunches (about $\frac{1}{4}$ lb) watercress
1$\frac{3}{4}$ oz butter
pepper
cayenne pepper
$\frac{1}{4}$ oz plain flour
$\frac{1}{2}$ pint good fish stock
1 teaspoon anchovy essence, or 2
  anchovies (pounded)
salt
lemon juice
1-2 oz cucumber (finely diced and
  blanched)

Method
Boil the watercress in salted water until just tender. Drain and sieve. Cream 1$\frac{1}{2}$ oz butter and work in watercress purée slowly. Add the pepper and a little cayenne. Make a roux with remaining butter and flour, stir in the stock with the anchovies and boil for 5 minutes. Skim, draw aside, then add the green butter gradually. Season, add the lemon juice and cucumber.

Turbot with fresh lobster sauce

3 lb piece of turbot

For court bouillon
2 pints water
1 teaspoon salt
9 peppercorns
1 onion (sliced)
1 carrot (sliced)
bouquet garni
1 tablespoon white wine vinegar,
   or juice of $\frac{1}{2}$ lemon

The turbot can be cooked and served 'in the piece' or you can, if preferred, order it from your fishmonger cut in even-size steaks.

Method
Put all the ingredients for the court bouillon in a pan and simmer, covered, for 8-10 minutes. Then cool and strain.

Soak the turbot for half an hour in cold salted water, then drain it and place, white side uppermost, in a pan or deep dish ready for poaching. Pour over the court bouillon and cook on top of stove, just below boiling point (allow about 10 minutes if cooking the fish in slices and 45-50 minutes if cooking it in the piece). Alternatively, poach in the oven pre-set at 350°F or Mark 4 (allowing 15 minutes for sliced fish).

Drain turbot well and dish up on a napkin. Serve with plainly boiled potatoes and the lobster sauce separately.

Lobster sauce

2 oz butter
2 oz lobster coral, or spawn
   (cooked)
salt and pepper
$\frac{3}{4}$ pint béchamel sauce (made with
   1$\frac{1}{4}$ oz butter, 1$\frac{1}{4}$ oz flour, $\frac{3}{4}$ pint
   flavoured milk)
diced cooked lobster meat from $\frac{1}{2}$
   lobster
1-2 tablespoons double cream

Method
Pound the butter with the cooked lobster coral, season and press through a nylon sieve. Prepare the béchamel sauce and, when boiling, draw it aside and beat in the lobster butter piece by piece. Add the lobster meat and finish with the cream.

Reheat but do not boil. Keep sauce hot in a bain-marie until it is wanted.

Adding lobster meat to béchamel sauce after beating in lobster butter

Dutch sauce

¾ pint milk (infused with 1 slice
  of onion, ½ bayleaf, 6 peppercorns)
1½ oz butter
1¼ oz plain flour
salt
2 egg yolks
juice of ½ lemon

Serve with fish croquettes.

Method
Strain flavoured milk into a bowl.
  Melt the butter in a small saucepan, remove from the heat and blend in the flour and strained milk. Add salt to taste and stir mixture over a gentle heat until boiling. Simmer for 1-2 minutes.
  Draw pan away from the heat, allow to cool very slightly then beat in the egg yolks. Reheat without boiling and add the lemon juice. Taste for seasoning. Use immediately.

Crab or lobster sauce

1 small can (approximately 3 oz)
  crab, or lobster meat
1 oz butter
scant oz plain flour
1 teaspoon paprika pepper
¼ pint fish stock (made from bones
  and trimmings of whiting)
¼ pint milk
1 tablespoon sherry
1 tablespoon double cream
salt and pepper

Serve with fish soufflé.

Method
Drain crab or lobster meat, break it up carefully with a fork, removing any membranes, and keep on one side.
  Melt butter in a pan, stir in flour and cook gently until honeycombed in appearance. Add paprika and cook for a few seconds (take care not to scorch it).
  Draw pan aside and blend in the stock, return pan to heat and stir until sauce begins to thicken ; then add milk and bring to boil. Cook for 2-3 minutes.
  Heat crab or lobster meat in sherry in a pan and add to sauce with the cream. Adjust seasoning.

Lobster salad Valencia with romesco sauce

2 live lobsters ($\frac{3}{4}$ lb each)
2 pints court bouillon
pinch of saffron
1 cucumber
salt
1 red and 1 green pepper
  (blanched)
1 lb tomatoes (skinned, seeds
  removed)
$\frac{1}{2}$ lb long grain rice

Method

Cook the lobsters in court bouillon for 15 minutes and allow to cool in the liquid.

Soak the saffron in a very little water; slice the cucumber and sprinkle with salt, cover and leave for about 30 minutes in a cool place. Shred the peppers and roughly chop the tomatoes.

Cook the rice in boiling water and the saffron liquid, drain, rinse and dry thoroughly.

Cut the lobster meat in neat, even-size pieces and mix with the rice and vegetables. Serve with romesco sauce.

Romesco sauce

4 tomatoes
2 cloves of garlic (peeled)
2 large red peppers
8-10 toasted almonds
salt
white pepper (ground from mill)
$\frac{1}{2}$ pint olive oil
wine vinegar (to taste)

Method

Bake the tomatoes, garlic and peppers in the oven, pre-set at 375°F or Mark 5, for 20-25 minutes or until soft. Remove the skin and seeds from the tomatoes and peppers and pound flesh to a smooth paste in a mortar with the garlic and almonds. Season, then add the oil, drop by drop, followed by the vinegar.

Allow the sauce to stand a little time to mellow, then strain and beat well before serving.

Court bouillon for shellfish

Slice 2 medium-size onions and a carrot, soften them slowly in $\frac{1}{2}$ oz butter, using a pan large enough to hold the shellfish. Add the juice of $\frac{1}{2}$ lemon, a large bouquet garni, 6 peppercorns, 2 pints water, $\frac{1}{4}$ pint white wine and 1 teaspoon salt. Simmer together for 15-20 minutes.

Mousseline sauce

2 egg yolks
3 oz unsalted butter
juice of $\frac{1}{2}$ lemon
salt and pepper
4 tablespoons double cream (lightly
   whipped)

Serve separately with salmon, lamb cutlets and asparagus. It is lighter, fluffier and more delicate than a hollandaise.

Method
Put the yolks into a bowl, add $\frac{1}{2}$ oz butter and stand bowl in a bain-marie. Work until mixture is thick, then add lemon juice and season lightly. Whisk over the bain-marie, add the remaining butter (slightly softened) by degrees.

When sauce is thick remove from heat and continue to whisk for 1-2 minutes. Then fold in the cream, adjust seasoning and serve.

Sweet pimiento sauce

2 small caps of canned pimiento
   (or 1 large one) — finely chopped
2 egg yolks
1 hard-boiled egg yolk (sieved)
$\frac{1}{2}$ teaspoon paprika pepper
salt and pepper
dash of Tabasco sauce
grated rind of $\frac{1}{2}$ orange
$7\frac{1}{2}$ fl oz olive, or salad, oil
about 1 dessertspoon vinegar
1 tablespoon juice from pimientos
1 tablespoon double cream

Serve with fish coated in batter and deep fried.

Method
Put the egg yolks, raw and hard-boiled, into a bowl. Work with the seasonings and orange rind, then gradually add the oil as for mayonnaise (see page 95). When it begins to get too thick, add the vinegar. When all the oil is mixed in, add the pimientos. Finish with juice and the cream and adjust seasoning.

A bain-marie provides the ideal gentle heat for thickening a delicate sauce

Tartare sauce

2 eggs (hard-boiled)
1 egg yolk (raw)
salt and pepper
$\frac{1}{2}$ pint oil
1 tablespoon vinegar
1 teaspoon chopped parsley
1 teaspoon snipped chives
1 teaspoon chopped capers, or
   gherkins

Serve with fried fish or fish croquettes.

Method
Cut the hard-boiled eggs in half, remove the yolks and rub them through a strainer into a bowl. Add the raw yolk and seasoning ; work well together. Add the oil drop by drop, as for a mayonnaise, and dilute with the vinegar as necessary. Finish off with the herbs and capers. If wished, add the shredded white of one of the hard-boiled eggs.

Ravigote sauce

$\frac{1}{2}$ pint sauce bâtarde (mock
  hollandaise) — see page 17
1 shallot (finely chopped)
2-3 tablespoons wine vinegar
$\frac{1}{2}$ oz butter
1 scant teaspoon French mustard
1 tablespoon chopped mixed herbs
  (tarragon, chives and parsley)

Serve with salmon, fried fish
and grilled pork chops.

Method
Prepare the mock hollandaise
sauce and set aside.

Simmer shallot in a pan in the
wine vinegar with the butter
until tender (2-3 minutes).
Add to the sauce bâtarde with
the mustard and herbs, reheat
gently.

This sauce should be slightly
sharp and well flavoured with
the herbs.

Maltaise sauce

3 egg yolks
3-4 oz unsalted butter
grated rind of $\frac{1}{2}$, and juice of 1,
  orange
salt and pepper
1 dessertspoon lemon juice
1 teaspoon tomato purée
3 tablespoons double cream (lightly
  whipped)

Method
Cream yolks in a bowl with $\frac{1}{2}$ oz
butter and grated orange rind ;
season. Stand bowl in a bain-
marie over heat ; add orange,
lemon juice and tomato purée.
Whisk until thick, adding rest of
the butter (slightly softened) by
degrees. Remove bowl from
heat, continue to whisk for a
minute, then fold in the cream.
Watchpoint In this sauce
there is a fair proportion of
liquid, so make sure this begins
to thicken before adding too
much of the butter. Quite a
strong heat is necessary to
start this off. Once the sauce
does begin to thicken, it will
happen quickly, so be ready to
take the bowl from the heat. The
butter can then be added fairly
rapidly.

Salmon cream with white wine sauce

1½ lb salmon (filleted, skinned
   and minced)
2 eggs (beaten)
2½ fl oz double cream

For panade
7½ fl oz milk
2 oz butter
2½ oz plain flour
salt and pepper

To garnish
1 cucumber
½ oz butter
salt and pepper
1 tablespoon chopped dill
   (optional)

*7-inch diameter cake tin, or 8-8½ inch
   diameter savarin mould*

Method
To make panade : bring milk to
the boil with butter, draw pan
aside, add the flour all at once
and beat until it is smooth.
Season panade and allow it to
cool. Pound the fish with the
panade (or work in blender)
then add the beaten eggs and
cream. Adjust the seasoning.
Fill cream into the buttered tin
or mould, cover with buttered
paper and then steam or poach
au bain-marie for about 40
minutes.

To prepare garnish : peel the
cucumber, cut in four lengthways, and trim into olive-shaped
pieces. Blanch pieces in pan of
boiling water for 1 minute,
drain and return them to pan
with ½ oz butter and seasoning
and simmer for 3-4 minutes
until tender ; finish with a little
chopped dill.

Turn the salmon cream on to
a hot serving dish, spoon over
the sauce and garnish with the
cucumber and /or dill.

White wine sauce 2

2 wineglasses white wine
1 shallot (finely chopped)
1¼ oz butter
1 oz plain flour
7½ fl oz fish stock
1 egg yolk
2½ fl oz double cream

Method
Put the wine and shallot in a
small pan and boil hard until
wine is reduced by half ; strain
it and keep on one side. Melt
the butter, add the flour and
cook very gently until it is
marbled in appearance and a
pale straw-colour ; draw pan
aside and blend in the stock
and wine. Season, return to the
heat and stir until sauce is
boiling ; simmer for 2-3 minutes.

Work the egg yolk and cream
together for a liaison and add
about 1 tablespoon of hot
sauce. Add the liaison very
slowly to sauce, then reheat
very carefully.

Venetian sauce

$\frac{1}{4}$-$\frac{1}{2}$ cucumber
handful of spinach
sprig of tarragon and chervil
2$\frac{1}{2}$ oz butter
scant $\frac{1}{2}$ oz plain flour
$\frac{1}{2}$ pint water
salt and pepper
2 egg yolks
2 shallots
3-4 tablespoons cooking liquor
   from fish (well reduced)

Serve with poached mackerel.

Method
Peel and dice cucumber ; blanch
for 3 minutes in a pan of boiling
water, then drain and set aside.
Cook spinach and herbs in a
pan of boiling salted water for
about 5 minutes. Then drain,
press out moisture and rub
through a wire strainer, or
mix in a blender.
   Melt $\frac{1}{2}$ oz butter in a pan and
stir in flour. Whisk in the water
with seasoning ; bring to boiling
point only and then draw aside ;
beat in egg yolks and remaining
butter, a small piece at a time.
Add spinach and herb purée and
adjust seasoning.
   Chop shallots finely, add
to strained cooking liquor from
fish and boil until liquid is
reduced to 3-4 tablespoons.
Strain this into the sauce, reheat
gently but do not boil. Add
cucumber and spoon over the
fish.

Genevoise sauce

2$\frac{1}{2}$ oz butter
scant $\frac{3}{4}$ oz plain flour
$\frac{1}{2}$ pint court bouillon (from fish it's
   being served with), or light stock
2 egg yolks
1-2 tablespoons cream, or top of
   milk
2-3 fillets of anchovy (soaked in
   milk) — optional
1$\frac{1}{2}$ teaspoons anchovy essence
pepper
1 dessertspoon chopped parsley

Serve with poached or grilled
fish.

Method
Melt about $\frac{3}{4}$ oz of butter in a
pan, stir in flour off the heat and
pour on court bouillon or stock.
Blend, return to heat and stir
until boiling. Leave to simmer for
2-3 minutes.
   Meanwhile mix egg yolks and
cream together in a basin ;
drain and crush anchovies
thoroughly with the essence
(fillets can be omitted and a
little more essence used).
   Draw sauce aside and pour a
little on to yolk mixture, stirring
well, then return by degrees to
pan. Beat in remaining butter in
small pieces with anchovies,
add pepper to taste and parsley.
Reheat carefully but do not boil.

Sauces for vegetables

The English way with vegetables tends to be boiled — and that's
that. The Cordon Bleu cook, though, can do so much more. Try a
delicious selection of vegetables in béchamel sauce as a main dish,
or one of the individual vegetable dishes as a starter. If you feel like
eating the French way, have your usual meat as a main course
but serve the vegetables separately afterwards and go to town with
a delicious sauce.
Don't forget that with vegetables, as with fish, the flavour of the
sauce must not overpower the whole dish ; also remember that
only first class, fresh vegetables will ever taste good, even if they are
buried under a delicious rich sauce.

Devilled mushrooms

$\frac{3}{4}$ lb mushrooms
1 oz butter
salt and pepper
squeeze of lemon juice
4 rounds of hot buttered toast
   (for serving)

Method
Trim and wash the mushrooms, dry them well, then fry very quickly in the butter for 1 minute. Season them well, adding a squeeze of lemon juice.

Remove the crusts from the toast, place slices in a gratin dish and arrange the mushrooms on the top.

Prepare devil sauce (see right). Spread devil mixture over the mushrooms and bake in a hot oven, pre-set at 425°F or Mark 7, for about 5-10 minutes until golden-brown on top.

Devil sauce

$\frac{1}{4}$ pint double cream
dash of Tabasco sauce
1 tablespoon tomato ketchup
1 teaspoon horseradish sauce
1 tablespoon Worcestershire sauce
squeeze of lemon juice
dash of freshly grated nutmeg
1 teaspoon French mustard

Method
To prepare devil mixture: lightly whip the cream, then carefully beat in all the seasonings until the mixture will hold its shape.

Mushrooms in devil sauce, served on hot toast, make a good savoury

Haricot beans with cream sauce

4 oz dried haricot beans
1 teaspoon bicarbonate of soda to 2 quarts boiling water (for soaking)
1 head of celery (sliced)
8 oz button onions
1 tablespoon chopped parsley

Method

Wash the beans in several changes of water. Pour on the boiling water (with bicarbonate of soda) and leave beans to soak overnight.

After soaking, rinse the beans well and place in a pan with celery and whole onions. Cover with cold water and bring very slowly to the boil. Simmer gently for about 1 hour until beans are tender.

Drain the vegetables and add to the sauce with the chopped parsley. Turn into a casserole for serving.

Cream sauce

For $\frac{3}{4}$ pint cream sauce
1$\frac{1}{2}$ oz butter
1$\frac{1}{2}$ oz plain flour
$\frac{3}{4}$ pint milk
salt and pepper
2-3 tablespoons single cream

Method

Make a roux with the flour and butter, add liquid off heat, season well and add the cream. Return to heat and boil.

Poulette sauce

$\frac{1}{2}$ pint velouté sauce
1 rounded teaspoon finely chopped parsley
1 teaspoon lemon juice
pinch of chopped savory

For liaison
1 egg yolk
2 tablespoons double cream

Serve with carrots, broad beans, new potatoes, or boiled veal. Half this quantity is enough for a dish of vegetables for 4-6 people.

Method

Add parsley, lemon juice and savory to velouté sauce. Mix thoroughly and boil. Make liaison by working egg yolk and cream together, add 1 tablespoon of hot sauce, then return this slowly to sauce; reheat carefully but do not reboil.

Cauliflower cream with duxelles sauce

1 large, or 2 small, cauliflowers
1 bayleaf
handful of large spinach leaves
$\frac{1}{2}$ pint duxelles sauce (for serving)

For panade
$7\frac{1}{2}$ fl oz béchamel sauce
salt and pepper
pinch of ground mace
2 eggs (one separated)
1 tablespoon cream

*7-8 inch diameter deep sandwich tin,
or 6-inch shallow cake tin*

Method
Break the cauliflower into sprigs, using a little of the green and all of the stalk. Cook these until tender, with bayleaf, in a pan of boiling salted water. Drain cauliflower well, remove the bayleaf, and pass through a sieve. Return cauliflower to the pan with a knob of butter. Set it over low heat to dry to a fairly firm purée. Stir purée occasionally, then set aside.

Meanwhile grease the tin. Dip the spinach leaves in boiling water for a few seconds to make them pliable. Drain them well and line them into the tin with the shiny side of the leaf next to the tin.

Prepare the béchamel sauce (if not already made).

Add the purée to the béchamel sauce, season well and add the mace ; beat in 1 whole egg and 1 yolk, reserving the white. Add the cream to sauce, whisk the white and fold it in. Turn cream at once into the prepared tin, cover it with buttered paper and steam or poach in a bain-marie for about 35-40 minutes or until firm to the touch.

A few minutes before turning cream out, take it off the heat or remove it from the oven and allow it to stand. After turning out, spoon round a little duxelles sauce and serve the rest separately.

Duxelles sauce

1 small onion, or shallot (finely chopped)
1 oz butter
3 oz dark flat mushrooms (washed and chopped)
scant oz plain flour
$\frac{1}{2}$ pint veal, or chicken, stock
salt and pepper
1 dessertspoon chopped mixed herbs

Method
Melt $\frac{1}{2}$ oz butter in a pan ; add the onion (or shallot) and cook for 3-4 minutes. Add the mushrooms and the rest of the butter to the pan. Cook for 3-4 minutes, stirring occasionally, then draw pan aside. Stir in the flour and add the stock. Return pan to the heat, stir until boiling, season well and add the herbs.

Potatoes in sauce indienne

1-1½ lb baby potatoes

For sauce indienne
1½ oz butter
1 shallot (finely chopped)
1 dessertspoon curry powder
1 oz plain flour
1 pint milk
salt and pepper
1 bayleaf

Method

Wash potatoes, plunge them into boiling water, cook them gently for 5 minutes, then drain and peel them.

Melt the butter in a pan, add the shallot and curry powder. Cook them gently for 1-2 minutes, then stir in the flour, add the milk, stir until it is boiling, season and cook gently for 3-4 minutes to reduce it slightly in quantity.

Add the bayleaf and the potatoes to sauce, shake the pan rather than stir to make sure that the potatoes are under the surface of the sauce. Cover the pan and continue to cook for about 7-8 minutes until potatoes are tender (this depends on the size of the potatoes). If it is more convenient, the potatoes and sauce may be put into a covered casserole and cooked in the oven at 350°F or Mark 4 for 7-8 minutes.

Note : this sauce is also good with eggs. Hardboil the eggs, shell and halve them. Make the sauce (omitting the potatoes), put in the eggs, cut side down. Spoon over the sauce and heat gently for a few minutes before serving.

Potatoes in sauce aurore

1-1½ lb baby potatoes
sprig of mint
¼ oz butter

For sauce aurore
½ lb fresh tomatoes, or 1 cup canned tomatoes
1 clove of garlic (crushed)
½ bayleaf
¼ oz butter
1-2 tablespoons cream

For béchamel sauce
1½ oz butter
1¼ oz plain flour
¾ pint flavoured milk
salt and pepper

This sauce is also good with fish and eggs.

Method

Scrape potatoes, put them into pan of boiling salted water with mint and simmer for 5-6 minutes.

Meanwhile, reduce the tomatoes to a thick pulp with the garlic, bayleaf and butter. When reduced, put tomato pulp through a strainer (this should yield about 4-5 fl oz).

Prepare the béchamel sauce, beat in strained tomato pulp, season to taste and finish with the cream. Drain the potatoes, add ¼ oz butter and pour over the sauce, shake the pan gently and continue to cook potatoes for 5-6 minutes, or until tender.

Sauces for meat

Brown sauces come into their own in this section, for although many white sauces are used with poultry or veal, the really delicious beef dishes often use a sauce that could be found in no other context.
To make the basic demi-glace (see page 14) is an art to start with, but if you can go on from there to produce some of the delicious sauces in this section, you will be a Cordon Bleu cook indeed.

Onion sauce

3 medium-size onions
1 oz butter
2 tablespoons plain flour
$\frac{1}{2}$ pint milk
salt and pepper
1 tablespoon double cream, or
$\frac{1}{2}$ oz butter (optional)

Method
Slice the onions and cook in boiling, salted water until tender. Drain thoroughly and sieve, or blend if you prefer a smooth sauce.

Melt the butter, take pan off the heat and add the flour. Tip on the scalded milk (scalding the milk will make it less likely to curdle) and, when thoroughly blended, stir continually over moderate heat until boiling. Simmer for 2-3 minutes, add the prepared onions, adjust seasoning and finish with a spoonful of cream or a knob of butter.

Mint sauce

2 tablespoons chopped fresh mint
1-2 tablespoons caster sugar
wine vinegar (to taste)

Method
Mint sauce should be bright green, smooth and pulpy in consistency. Pound the chopped mint with a little of the caster sugar until quite smooth. Add 1-2 tablespoons boiling water, according to the quantity of mint, to improve the colour and melt the sugar. Add a little wine vinegar to taste.

Redcurrant jelly

It is not possible to give a specific quantity of redcurrants as the recipe is governed by the amount of juice made, which is variable.

Method
Wash the fruit and, without removing from the stems, put in a 7 lb jam jar or stone crock. Cover and stand in deep pan of hot water. Simmer on top of the stove or in the oven, pre-set at 350°F or Mark 4, mashing the fruit a little from time to time, until all the juice is extracted (about 1 hour).

Then turn fruit into a jelly-bag, or double linen strainer, and allow to drain undisturbed overnight over a basin.
Watchpoint To keep the jelly clear and sparkling, do not try to speed up the draining process by forcing juice through ; this will only make the jelly cloudy.

Now measure juice. Allowing 1 lb lump or preserving sugar to each pint of juice, mix juice and sugar together, dissolving over slow heat. When dissolved, bring to the boil, boil hard for 3-5 minutes and skim with a wooden spoon. Test a little on a saucer : allow jelly to cool, tilt saucer and, if jelly is set, it will wrinkle. Put into jam jars, place small circles of greaseproof paper over jelly, label and cover with jam pot covers. Store in a dry larder until required.

Loin of lamb portugaise with lemon sauce

2½-3 lb loin of lamb (chined)
1½ pints water
1 tablespoon instant browned onions
1 carrot
bouquet garni
salt and pepper
1-2 oz butter
1 wineglass white wine
bunch of watercress (to garnish)

Fine string and trussing needle, or poultry pins

Method
First make the stock : remove the chine bone and any small chop bones from the lamb and put these in a pan with the water, onion, carrot, bouquet garni and seasoning and simmer for 45-50 minutes ; strain and then reduce the liquid to ½ pint. Set oven at 400 °F or Mark 6.

Prepare a walnut and lemon stuffing (see page 126).

Spread the lamb with the stuffing, roll up and secure with poultry pins and fine string (or sew up using fine string and a trussing needle). Score the surface of the lamb and rub with the butter and set in a roasting tin ; pour round the wine, cover with a buttered paper and roast for about 1¼ hours in pre-set oven, basting from time to time. After 40 minutes, turn the meat and remove the buttered paper.

Meanwhile prepare the sauce.

Take up the meat and keep it warm. Tip off the fat from the roasting tin and strain the remaining sediment into the sauce. Carve the meat and arrange it on a hot serving dish. Skim the sauce well and add the chopped mint ; spoon a little sauce over the meat to keep it moist and serve the rest in a sauce boat.

Lemon sauce

1 oz butter
scant oz plain flour
½ pint stock
1 tablespoon redcurrant jelly
juice of ½ lemon and ½ orange
1 tablespoon chopped mint

Method
Melt the butter, stir in the flour and cook slowly until russet-brown. Draw the pan aside, pour on the stock, add the redcurrant jelly and fruit juices and blend until smooth. Season well and stir over gentle heat until boiling, then keep the sauce simmering.

Loin of lamb portugaise, garnished with watercress. A little of the sauce is spooned over the meat and the remainder is served separately

Barbecue sauce 1

1 teaspoon plain flour
⅓ pint potato stock (water in which
   potatoes have been cooked)
1 tablespoon soy sauce
dash of Worcestershire sauce
salt and pepper
2 tomatoes

This sauce goes well with lamb kebabs or pork chops.

Method

Skim off the fat from the grill pan in which you have cooked your meat, leaving about 1 dessertspoon and any sediment. Stir in flour and cook very gently for 2-3 minutes. Draw aside and blend in potato stock, sauces and seasoning, then return to heat and stir until boiling. Skin the tomatoes, cut the flesh into shreds and add to mixture. Simmer for 1 minute.

Barbecue sauce 2

2 tablespoons tomato ketchup
2 tablespoons mushroom ketchup
2 tablespoons Worcestershire sauce
1-2 tablespoons bottled spicy fruit
   sauce, or 1-2 tablespoons home-
   made red plum or gooseberry
   spicy fruit sauce
1-2 oz butter (melted)
1 teaspoon sugar
dash of red wine vinegar
dash of Tabasco sauce

Method

Add all the sauces to the melted butter, sugar, vinegar and Tabasco and mix.

Mix these bottled sauces together to give your lamb a barbecue tang

Sauce piquante

1 shallot (finely chopped)
$\frac{1}{2}$ oz butter
scant $\frac{1}{2}$ oz plain flour
$7\frac{1}{2}$-10 fl oz good brown stock
1 teaspoon tomato purée
salt and pepper
1 dessertspoon finely chopped
  gherkins
squeeze of lemon juice
1 dessertspoon finely chopped
  parsley
$\frac{1}{4}$ oz butter

Method

Lightly brown the shallot in the butter, stir in the flour, cook for $\frac{1}{2}$ minute and then draw pan aside. Add the stock to pan, blend in the tomato purée and bring sauce to the boil ; simmer it for 10 minutes until syrupy, season and add the gherkins. Draw pan aside, add the lemon juice, parsley and, lastly, the butter. Stir sauce well and reheat, but do not boil.

Note : if, once the sauce has simmered, it is thicker than a gravy, add a little more stock.

Provençal sauce

2 oz button mushrooms
2 shallots
1 clove of garlic
1 tablespoon oil
1 dessertspoon plain flour
1 wineglass strong stock
1 wineglass white wine
salt and pepper
bouquet garni
1 teaspoon tomato purée

Method

Peel the mushrooms, cut the stalks level with the caps and chop both peelings and stalks very finely with the shallots and garlic.

Heat the oil, add the mushroom and shallot mixture and cook gently for 5 minutes until the shallot just begins to colour.

Dust in the flour, moisten with the stock and wine and stir until boiling. Season and add bouquet garni, simmer for 20 minutes, then strain. Return the sauce to the rinsed pan, add the tomato purée and the mushroom caps, cut in slices. Simmer for 2-3 minutes.

Tournedos chasseur with mushroom sauce

5 tournedos
1 oz butter (for frying)
5 slices of bread for croûtes
 (about $\frac{1}{4}$ inch thick)
oil and butter (for frying
 croûtes)
1 wineglass white wine
1 teaspoon chopped tarragon
1 tablespoon chopped parsley

Method

First prepare the sauce.

Trim bread for croûtes to the same size as tournedos. Fry croûtes in butter and oil and keep hot. Heat the butter in a large frying pan and put in tournedos. Fry over quick heat, 3 minutes on each side ; place each tournedos on a croûte and arrange them on a serving dish.

Drain away any butter from the pan, deglaze it with the white wine. Boil wine quickly for 1-2 minutes to reduce, then add the mushroom sauce and reboil. Cook for 1-2 minutes. Add the chopped herbs to the sauce and spoon it over the tournedos. Serve very hot.

Mushroom sauce

3 oz button mushrooms
1 oz butter
2 shallots (finely chopped)
1 dessertspoon plain flour
$7\frac{1}{2}$ fl oz strong stock (preferably
 jellied)
1 rounded teaspoon tomato purée
salt and pepper

Method

Trim the mushrooms by cutting off the ends of the stalks level with the caps ; wash, dry and cut caps in fine slices. Heat a small frying or sauté pan, add the butter, then mushrooms, and sauté quickly until lightly coloured. Add the chopped shallot and cook gently for a few minutes, taking care it does not burn. Stir in flour and, after a few seconds, add stock and purée, and season lightly. Stir sauce until boiling, then simmer gently for 10-15 minutes.

Fondue bourguignonne

A fondue bourguignonne is a perfect choice for a casual party, and while a true bourguignonne is always prepared with fillet steak this expensive cut can be augmented with prawns / scampi and chicken breasts.

A 'fondue set' is essential as guests cook their own meat in hot oil and then dip it into bowls of sauces and relishes of their choice. A fondue set consists of a flameproof pot with a lid and stand, used over a spirit burner. Long-handled fondue forks prevent burning your hands when dipping the chosen food into the hot oil. Remember that the meat must be transferred to another fork for eating, to prevent burning the mouth.

Choose a hollandaise or béarnaise sauce and 3 or 4 of those given here for a really good selection. Plenty of French bread should be supplied and, on the side, large bowls of tossed green salad and a choice of two or three cheeses.

Sauces

Tomato devil sauce

4 large ripe tomatoes
4 tablespoons tomato ketchup
1 tablespoon red wine vinegar
2 tablespoons oil
few drops of Tabasco sauce
salt and pepper
dry mustard

Method
Skin the tomatoes, cut in half, remove seeds, and chop the flesh coarsely. Mix with the other ingredients and serve cold.

Sweet and sour sauce

1 green pepper
1 can (13½ oz) crushed pineapple
1 tablespoon honey
1 tablespoon red wine vinegar
1 tablespoon soy sauce
¼ pint soured cream
¼ pint boiled dressing (see page 93)
salt and pepper
squeeze of lemon juice

Method
Remove the core and seeds of the pepper and chop the flesh coarsely. Drop into boiling salted water and cook for 1 minute, drain and refresh. When cold, mix with the pineapple.

Stir the honey, vinegar and soy sauce into the soured cream, and boiled dressing, add the blanched pepper and pineapple ; season. Add lemon juice to taste.

Horseradish sauce

1 dessertspoon freshly grated horseradish
½ oz butter
½ oz plain flour
¼ pint chicken stock
¼ pint single cream
dash of cayenne pepper
salt and pepper
squeeze of lemon juice

Method
Melt the butter in a pan, blend in the flour and cook for 2-3 minutes. Add the chicken stock, stir until boiling and then cook for 3 minutes. Add the horseradish and cream and reboil. Season with salt and pepper and cayenne and add the lemon juice. Serve hot.

Fondue bourguignonne continued

Mustard cream

2 teaspoons Dijon mustard
$\frac{1}{4}$ pint mayonnaise (see page 95)
$\frac{1}{4}$ pint soured cream
salt and pepper
squeeze of lemon juice

Method
Mix the mustard into the mayonnaise, add the soured cream, seasoning and a few drops of lemon juice.

Cumberland sauce

1 orange
4 tablespoons redcurrant jelly
juice of $\frac{1}{2}$ lemon
1 glass port wine

Method
Remove rind from a quarter of the orange with a potato peeler. Cut into needle-like shreds and cook in boiling water until tender, then drain and rinse well. Heat the redcurrant jelly until dissolved, then stir in the lemon juice, wine and strained juice of the orange. When cold, add the orange rind and serve.

(This sauce is also good served with boiled ham.)

Fondue bourguignonne is shown here with Cumberland, hollandaise and tomato devil sauce, anchovy mayonnaise and horseradish sauce

Béarnaise sauce

3 tablespoons wine vinegar
6 peppercorns
$\frac{1}{2}$ bayleaf
1 blade of mace
1 slice of onion
2 egg yolks
salt and pepper
3-4 oz unsalted butter
nut of meat glaze, or jelly at base
   of cake of beef dripping
1 teaspoon chopped tarragon,
   chervil, and parsley
pinch of snipped chives, or grated
   onion

This quantity is sufficient to put
on steaks or cutlets but ingredients should be increased in
proportion for a sauce to be
served separately.

Method

Put the vinegar, peppercorns,
bayleaf, mace and slice of
onion into a small pan and boil
until reduced to 1 tablespoon.
Set pan aside.

Place the yolks in a small
basin and beat well with a pinch
of salt and $\frac{1}{2}$ oz butter. Strain
on vinegar mixture and set the
bowl on a pan of boiling water,
turn off heat and stir until beginning to thicken.

Add the softened butter in
small pieces, each about the
size of a hazelnut, stirring all the
time. Season with pepper. Add
the meat glaze, herbs, and
chives or grated onion. Keep
warm and use as required.

The finished sauce should
have the consistency of whipped
cream.

Sauce bordelaise

2 shallots (finely chopped)
2 wineglasses claret
1 small sprig of thyme
$\frac{1}{4}$ bayleaf
$\frac{3}{4}$ pint demi-glace sauce (preferably
   made with veal bone stock)
little extra bone stock
1 teaspoon arrowroot (mixed with 1
   tablespoon stock)
1-2 marrow bones, or $\frac{3}{4}$ oz butter

Serve with beef roasts or grills.

Method

Put shallots, wine and herbs into
a pan, simmer to reduce by
about one-third, then add to
prepared demi-glace sauce.
Bring to boil and simmer for
6-7 minutes, skimming well.
Add a dash of cold stock to
help skimming. When you have
a good, concentrated flavour
thicken, if necessary, with
arrowroot. Strain into a clean
pan and keep warm.

With a knife dipped in hot
water, scoop marrow from
marrow bone and cut into small
dice. Poach for 6-7 minutes in
water just on boil. Drain carefully on a piece of muslin or
absorbent paper. Add to sauce
just before serving.

If not using marrow bones,
briskly stir in butter in small
pieces just before serving.

Meat balls with tomato and pepper sauce

1 lb minced raw beef
6 oz minced raw pork
1 cup (3 oz) fine dried breadcrumbs
2 oz grated Parmesan cheese
1 tablespoon chopped parsley
2 cloves of garlic (crushed with salt)
salt and pepper
2 eggs (beaten)
scant $\frac{1}{4}$ pint milk
seasoned flour
3 tablespoons dripping, or oil

For sauce
2 large onions (chopped)
1 oz plain flour
1 can (14 oz) tomatoes
2 green peppers (core and seeds removed, flesh chopped)
salt, pepper and sugar (to taste)
dash of Worcestershire sauce
1 bayleaf

Method
Mix the meat, breadcrumbs, cheese, parsley, garlic, and seasonings, and bind with the beaten eggs and milk. Shape mixture into $1\frac{1}{2}$-inch balls and roll them in seasoned flour.

Melt about 3 tablespoons good dripping (or oil) in a pan and fry the meat balls a few at a time until golden-brown on all sides. Remove balls and keep warm.

To make sauce, add the onions to the pan and cook slowly until golden. Blend in the flour, followed by the remaining ingredients, and stir until boiling. Replace the meat balls, cover and simmer for 1 hour. Serve with plainly boiled spaghetti, tossed in butter and seasoned, allowing 2 oz pasta per person.

Sauce chasseur

$7\frac{1}{2}$ fl oz demi-glace sauce
3 oz mushrooms (finely sliced)
little oil, or butter
2 shallots (chopped)
$2\frac{1}{2}$ fl oz white wine
1 dessertspoon tomato purée
$\frac{1}{2}$ oz butter
little parsley and 2 leaves of tarragon (chopped)

Method
Fry the mushrooms lightly in oil or butter ; when just browned, add the shallots and cook for 1-2 minutes, then add the white wine. Reduce the wine to half its quantity, then stir in the tomato purée and the demi-glace sauce. Simmer sauce for 1-2 minutes, remove pan from the heat, add the butter in small pieces and the chopped herbs. Serve at once.

Sauce espagnole

2 oz mushrooms (chopped)
1 rounded tablespoon tomato purée
$\frac{3}{4}$ pint demi-glace sauce
$2\frac{1}{2}$ fl oz jelled stock
$2\frac{1}{2}$ fl oz brown sherry
$\frac{1}{2}$ oz butter

Method
Put mushrooms in tomato purée and add both to prepared demi-glace sauce in a pan. Simmer for 5 minutes, then add stock. Continue to simmer, skimming often, until well reduced, then add sherry and beat in butter. Do not boil after this but keep warm in a bain-marie or reheat when necessary.

Apple sauce

1 lb cooking apples
rind of $\frac{1}{2}$ lemon
1 dessertspoon caster sugar
$\frac{1}{2}$ oz butter

Method

Peel and core the apples. Pare the lemon rind thinly. Put apples and rind in a saucepan with 2-3 tablespoons water. Cover tightly and cook until pulpy. Beat with a wooden spoon until smooth, or put through a strainer. Stir in the sugar and butter. Serve hot.

Apple and cider sauce

1 lb cooking apples
rind of $\frac{1}{2}$ lemon (thinly pared)
2-3 tablespoons cider
1 dessertspoon caster sugar
$\frac{1}{2}$ oz butter

Method

Prepare as for apple sauce (above) but cook apples in 2-3 tablespoons cider instead of water.

Parsley sauce

2 large handfuls of fresh parsley
$\frac{3}{4}$ pint milk
1 bayleaf
1 blade of mace
6 peppercorns
1$\frac{1}{2}$ oz butter
2 rounded tablespoons plain flour
salt and pepper

Serve with boiled chicken and also with ham, fish and eggs.

Method

To prepare the sauce : pick parsley sprigs from stalks and wash well ; reserve some stalks. Boil sprigs for 7 minutes in a saucepan of salted water, drain, press and rub through a bowl strainer to make about 1 dessertspoon of parsley purée.

Meanwhile infuse the milk with the bayleaf, mace, peppercorns, reserved parsley stalks. Strain. Melt the butter, stir in flour off the heat, blend in milk, return to heat and stir until boiling. Season and simmer for 2-3 minutes, then add the parsley purée.

Chaudfroid sauce (white)

1 oz butter
1 oz plain flour
$\frac{3}{4}$ pint flavoured milk (as for a béchamel)
2-3 tablespoons double cream
salt and pepper
1 wineglass aspic jelly (made with veal, chicken or fish stock)
good $\frac{1}{4}$ oz gelatine

This quantity is sufficient for a large chicken chaudfroid or chicken galantine. Any that is left over can be kept for a future occasion, or, if only small in quantity, it can be added to a béchamel for a hot dish or for a soup.

Method

Melt the butter, remove from heat, stir in the flour and strain on the milk. Blend and stir over the heat until boiling. Add the cream, season and simmer for 1-2 minutes, draw aside and cover with a piece of foil or damp greaseproof paper and the lid to prevent a skin forming. Allow to cool.

Dissolve the gelatine in the aspic and stir into the sauce. Wring sauce through a tammy cloth or muslin and use when it is on the point of setting.

Note : if using a velouté sauce as a base, take $\frac{1}{2}$ pint of strong stock, either chicken, veal or fish, and $\frac{1}{4}$ pint of double cream instead of the milk and cream quantities given above.

The roux, aspic and gelatine remain the same quantities as those given above.

Chaudfroid sauce (brown)

$\frac{3}{4}$ pint well reduced demi-glace, or brown, sauce
1 glass golden sherry
1 teaspoon tomato purée (optional)
1 sherry glass aspic (made with veal, or beef, or game, stock)
$\frac{1}{2}$ oz gelatine

Method

Make the demi-glace sauce, add the sherry to it and boil gently for 2-3 minutes. Draw aside, cool and add the gelatine dissolved in the aspic, then wring through a tammy strainer or cloth. Leave to cool, covered as for white chaudfroid. Use when cool and on the point of setting.

Watchpoint It is essential that the colour and flavour of the brown sauce should be the best possible. If necessary, add 1 teaspoon of tomato purée to it with the sherry ; this will improve both the colour and the flavour.

A tammy strainer is made of very fine double-mesh wire. When a sauce is strained through a tammy strainer, it becomes very smooth and acquires a high gloss as a result of emulsification. It is more usual to use this strainer than a tammy cloth, which is a rough-textured material like a coarse flannel.

Tomato chaudfroid sauce

$\frac{3}{4}$ oz butter
$\frac{3}{4}$ oz plain flour
$\frac{1}{2}$ pint flavoured milk (as for béchamel)
2-3 tablespoons double cream
salt and pepper
1 wineglass aspic jelly
good $\frac{1}{4}$ oz gelatine

For tomato pulp
$\frac{1}{2}$ lb ripe tomatoes, or 1 cup canned Italian tomatoes
bouquet garni
1 clove of garlic

Method
First make tomato pulp. Halve the tomatoes, squeeze to remove seeds and cook flesh to a pulp with bouquet garni and the clove of garlic, left whole.

Rub the reduced mixture through a strainer or piece of muslin ; it should make 1 wineglass of pulp. Make up the sauce as for a white chaudfroid (see previous page), first making the béchamel or velouté sauce, then adding the pulp and seasoning to taste before stirring gelatine and aspic into the sauce.

A chaudfroid takes its name from the sauce. It is always used for a cold dish — the hot sauce being left to go cold before coating the cold cooked food. White or tomato chaudfroid are coated over chicken, eggs and white meat. Brown chaudfroid is used for game.

Bread sauce

4-6 tablespoons fresh white breadcrumbs
$\frac{1}{2}$ pint milk
1 small onion (stuck with 2-3 cloves)
$\frac{1}{2}$ bayleaf
salt and pepper
1 oz butter

Method
Bring the milk to the boil, add onion and bayleaf, cover pan and leave on the side of the stove for at least 15 minutes to infuse. Remove onion and bayleaf, add breadcrumbs and seasoning and return to the heat. Stir gently until boiling, then remove from heat. Beat in butter, a small piece at a time. Serve hot.

Cranberry sauce

1 lb cranberries
1 teacup cold water
4 oz granulated sugar
about 1 tablespoon port
    (optional)

Method
Wash the cranberries and put them in a saucepan, cover with cold water and bring to the boil. Simmer, bruising the cranberries with a wooden spoon, until reduced to a pulp.

Add sugar and port (if using). Cook very gently until all the sugar is dissolved.

Bigarade sauce

2 shallots (finely chopped)
nut of butter
1 wineglass red wine
small bayleaf
rind and juice of 1 orange
    (preferably Seville)
$\frac{1}{2}$ pint demi-glace sauce
1 teaspoon redcurrant jelly (see
    page 37)

Serve with duck, venison, pork or braised tongue.

Method
Chop the shallots finely and soften them in butter in a small pan. Add the wine and bayleaf. Reduce gently by about one-third. Add to the demi-glace sauce, together with the juice and half the pared orange rind. Simmer for 5-7 minutes.

Shred remaining orange rind thinly, blanch for 5 minutes, and drain. Strain sauce and return to pan with shredded rind and redcurrant jelly. Bring slowly to boil, stirring frequently to dissolve the jelly.

Note : to be correct, a small bitter or Seville orange should be used for this sauce. If, however, a sweet one has to be used, sharpen the sauce with a few drops of lemon juice.

Raisin sauce

4 oz seeded raisins (cut in
   small pieces)
8 oz granulated sugar
$\frac{1}{4}$ pint water
1 oz butter
1 tablespoon Worcestershire
   sauce
3 tablespoons wine vinegar
a few drops of Tabasco sauce
salt and pepper
small pinch of ground mace
4 oz redcurrant jelly (see page 37)

Method
Dissolve the sugar in the water
and boil steadily for 5 minutes.
Add all the other ingredients
and simmer gently until the
redcurrant jelly has dissolved.
Serve this hot with baked ham.

Braised ham madère

1 gammon slipper (about $1\frac{1}{2}$ lb),
   or small corner piece of
   gammon($2\frac{1}{2}$-3 lb)
2 onions
2 carrots
small piece of turnip
1 stick of celery
1 oz butter
1 glass Madeira, or sherry
   (optional)
$\frac{1}{4}$ pint jellied stock
bouquet garni
salt and pepper

Method
Soak gammon in cold water for
12 hours, then drain and parboil
it in fresh water : 30 minutes for
a slipper, 1 hour for a corner
piece. Set oven at 325°F or
Mark 3. Slice vegetables and
cook gently in butter, drain ham
and place on top.

Pour over 1 glass of Madeira
or sherry, if used, and set alight
to drive off alcohol. Add stock,
bouquet garni and seasoning.
Cover with greaseproof paper
and lid, braise gently in oven
for 1 hour.

Prepare sauce (see right).

Skin and slice ham, arrange
on serving dish on a bed of
spinach à la crème, spoon over
the sauce and serve with
creamed potatoes, or with new
potatoes tossed in butter and
chopped parsley.

The braising juice, if not too
fat or salty, may be reduced and
added to the sauce.

Sauce madère

2 tablespoons oil, or dripping
1 rounded tablespoon plain flour
1¼ pint clear brown jellied stock
  (flavoured with vegetables)
½ teaspoon tomato purée
1 glass Madeira, or golden sherry

Tammy strainer

To prepare sauce : melt fat, stir in flour and cook until straw coloured, add stock and tomato purée. Simmer for at least 45 minutes, skimming frequently. When well reduced and clear, strain sauce through a tammy strainer, boil the Madeira or sherry to reduce by half and add to the sauce.

Braised ham is sliced and served on a bed of spinach à la crème with rich sauce madère poured over it ; creamed or new potatoes accompany it

Koftas (meat balls in curry sauce)

1 lb finely minced lamb, or
   chicken (raw)
$\frac{1}{2}$ green pepper
1 medium-size onion
1 clove of garlic (crushed with salt)
$2\frac{1}{2}$ fl oz plain yoghourt
2 tablespoons chopped coriander
salt
2 teaspoons garam masala
$\frac{1}{4}$ teaspoon ground mace
1 egg (beaten)

Method
Chop the green pepper and
onion very finely. Mix all the
ingredients with enough beaten
egg to bind firmly. Form
into balls about $1\frac{1}{2}$ inches in
diameter, then simmer them in
the curry sauce for 30 minutes.

Curry sauce

1 medium-size onion (finely
   sliced)
2 tablespoons melted butter
2 medium-size tomatoes
   (skinned and chopped)
2 cloves of garlic (crushed)
2 teaspoons curry powder
1-inch piece of green ginger
   (scraped and finely chopped)
pinch of cayenne pepper
1 teaspoon salt
$\frac{1}{2}$ pint plain yoghourt
$\frac{1}{4}$ pint hot water (optional)

Method
Fry the onions in the butter until
a pale gold. Add the tomatoes,
garlic and curry powder. Fry
gently for 2-3 minutes. Stir in
the ginger, cayenne and salt,
then mix in the yoghourt and
simmer for 15 minutes. If a
thinner sauce is required, add
the hot water. Adjust seasoning.

Sauces for pasta

No pasta dish can survive without a good sauce. One of the most popular is tomato, and we have given several variations in this section. Sometimes the sauce is the only accompaniment to the noodles, spooned on top ; at others the pasta is mixed lightly with a sauce and another, more substantial item such as meat balls is served with it.

Both sauces and meat with pasta should be rich and piquant in flavour, to contrast with the blandness of the pasta. Each of these recipes can be served in small quantities as a starter, or in larger quantities as a main course.

Basic tomato sauce

1 oz butter
1 rounded dessertspoon plain flour
$\frac{1}{2}$ pint stock, or water
1 lb tomatoes, or 1 can (15 oz)
  tomatoes
bouquet garni
salt and pepper
pinch of granulated sugar (to
  season)
1 teaspoon tomato purée (optional)

Method

Melt the butter in a pan, stir in the flour. Draw pan off the heat, blend in the stock or water, return to heat and stir until boiling.

Cut the tomatoes in half (after wiping them if fresh), and squeeze to remove seeds. Strain seeds to obtain juice only. Place tomatoes and juice into the sauce and add bouquet garni. Season and add tomato purée to strengthen flavour if necessary. Cover pan and cook gently for 25-35 minutes until tomatoes are pulpy. Remove bouquet garni and turn sauce into a strainer. Press it through, return to the rinsed-out pan, adjust seasoning and boil gently for about 5 minutes or until it is the right consistency.

Watchpoint A tomato sauce must have a flowing consistency as opposed to a coating one. The appearance is improved by stirring in $\frac{1}{2}$ oz butter just before serving. This will give the sauce a good gloss.

Bottled tomato sauce

7 lb tomatoes
2 rounded tablespoons salt
2 large cooking apples
3 large onions (chopped)
1 pint white malt, or white
  wine, vinegar
$\frac{1}{2}$ lb granulated sugar
1 dessertspoon pepper
1 dessertspoon cloves
1 dessertspoon ground mace

Method

Wipe and slice tomatoes, lay in a dish and sprinkle with the salt. Leave for 1-2 hours. Quarter, core and roughly chop the apples ; put these into a preserving pan with the onions, vinegar, sugar and spices and bring to the boil. Now put in tomatoes and simmer very gently for $1\frac{1}{2}$-2 hours ; the mixture should be well flavoured and pulpy. Pass it through a sieve or work in a blender. Rinse out the pan, pour back the mixture and simmer until it is the consistency of cream. This may take about 30 minutes. Leave until cold, then pour into clean, dry sauce bottles and screw down lids well.

Tomato sauce

(For pasta 'al sugo')

1 lb tomatoes, or 1 can (15 oz)
1 small onion (sliced)
1 oz butter, or 2 tablespoons oil
1 clove of garlic (chopped)
good pinch of dried mixed herbs
1 wineglass stock, or water
salt and pepper
tomato purée
$\frac{1}{2}$ oz butter

This sauce, which is almost a purée, is made without any thickening, but is so reduced that it is red-brown in colour and on the point of 'breaking' (curdling). It is this reduction which gives it its characteristic strong and piquant flavour. This sauce goes very well with spaghetti.

Method

Wipe tomatoes, cut in half and squeeze out seeds. Slice and put into a pan with the onion, 1 oz butter (or oil) and garlic. Add herbs and stock or water, season well, cover and cook to a pulp. Rub through a strainer, return to the rinsed-out pan and add a little tomato purée to strengthen the flavour. Use your own judgment as to the amount, as this depends on the ripeness of the tomatoes. Add the $\frac{1}{2}$ oz butter and boil until thick, stirring frequently.

When tomatoes are plentiful a double quantity (or more) can be made as it will keep for about a week in a covered container in the refrigerator, or can be deep frozen.

Bolognese sauce 1

2 tablespoons oil, or 1 oz butter
4 oz chicken livers (approximately 3)
1 medium-size onion (sliced)
1 clove of garlic (chopped)
1 rounded dessertspoon plain flour
3 teaspoons tomato purée
$\frac{1}{2}$ pint beef stock (or equivalent made from beef bouillon cube)
1 tablespoon Marsala, or brown sherry
salt and pepper
chopped parsley
Parmesan cheese (grated)

This sauce is best spooned over rather than mixed in with the spaghetti. Cook spaghetti in plenty of boiling water until just tender, drain, rinse and finish with oil or butter. Turn into serving dish and spoon the sauce in a band over the top. Serve grated Parmesan cheese separately. Bolognese sauce should be made with chicken livers but lamb's liver can be substituted although it does not give the same piquant flavour.

Method

Heat oil (or butter) in a shallow saucepan, put in the livers, sauté for 3-4 minutes until 'seized' and nicely brown. Take out, add the onion and garlic, sauté until turning colour, then stir in the flour, add purée, stock and Marsala or sherry. Stir until boiling. Simmer for 10 minutes, then add liver, coarsely chopped.

Continue to simmer until thick and syrupy for a further 7-10 minutes. Adjust seasoning and spoon sauce over the spaghetti. Sprinkle well with chopped parsley.

Bolognese sauce 2

2-3 tablespoons oil
1 medium-size onion (chopped)
2 oz mushrooms (sliced)
¼ lb raw beef (finely minced)
1 rounded dessertspoon tomato
purée
pinch of dried oregano
1 clove of garlic (crushed with salt)
¼ of a green pepper (chopped) —
optional
7½ fl oz stock

Method

Soften onion in the oil, add the mushrooms, the mince, purée, oregano, crushed clove of garlic and green pepper if used.

Fry mixture for a few minutes, then stir in the stock. Season, cover and simmer for 25-30 minutes or until meat is tender. If sauce gets too thick add a little more stock. Spoon sauce over cooked spaghetti.

Milanese sauce

4 oz mushrooms (sliced)
½ oz butter
½ pint strong, well-flavoured
tomato sauce
4 oz lean cooked ham (shredded)

This sauce is excellent to serve with spaghetti or any type of pasta, especially when served as a main course. In this case extra ham and mushrooms can be added as in this recipe. Otherwise, it is only necessary to use 2 oz each of mushrooms and ham to ½ pint tomato sauce.

Method

Sauté mushrooms in the butter for 3-4 minutes, then add the sauce. Simmer for a few minutes, then add the ham. Have ready the spaghetti cooked, well drained and mixed with ½ oz butter. Add the sauce and toss up over heat. Serve with grated Parmesan cheese.

Napolitana sauce

1 oz butter, or 2 tablespoons oil
1 medium-size onion (thinly
  sliced)
1 dessertspoon plain flour
1 wineglass stock
1 lb ripe tomatoes (skinned, the
  stalk cut out and the tomatoes
  lightly squeezed to remove seeds)
1 clove of garlic (crushed with salt)
1 teaspoon tomato conserve, or
  purée
1 bayleaf
pinch of sugar
salt
pepper (ground from mill)

This tomato sauce is not reduced as much as that in the
'al sugo' recipe, and is rougher
in texture. Serve mixed with, or
over, the pasta, or if preferred
the pasta and sauce can all be
turned into a gratin dish and
browned in the oven.

Method
Melt butter or oil in a shallow
saucepan, add onion, fry gently
for 3-4 minutes, then stir in
flour and add stock. Bring to the
boil. Slice tomatoes and add
with the garlic, conserve or
purée, bayleaf, sugar, salt and
pepper.
   Simmer for 25-30 minutes or
until well reduced to a thick
rich pulp. Remove bayleaf. Have
the pasta ready, put in a serving
dish and spoon the sauce over
the top.

Macaroni cheese

6 oz macaroni
grated cheese (for topping)
½ pint mornay sauce (see page 18)
extra milk (optional)

A creamy mornay sauce goes
specially well with the larger
pasta, such as this, which can
be served just mixed with the
sauce, or gratiné, ie. tipped into
a gratin dish and browned to a
crisp golden crust in the oven.

Method
Break macaroni in half and
lower into plenty of boiling
salted water. Stir once with a
wooden fork or spoon. Simmer
until tender (about 20 minutes ;
macaroni should be cooked a
little more than spaghetti), then
drain in a colander. Pour over
1-2 cups of hot water, drain
again well, then tip back into
the saucepan, cover and keep
warm while making the sauce.
   Prepare mornay sauce and
season well. Add sauce to the
macaroni, stir gently to mix, then
turn into a gratin dish. Grate
cheese on top to cover fairly
thickly then brown in the oven
at 400°F or Mark 6 for about 15
minutes.
Watchpoint For a good macaroni
cheese there must be ample
sauce — add a little extra milk
if sauce is too thick after the
addition of the cheese.

Savoury butters

Serve savoury butters with grilled meat and fish. Take the cut direct from the grill, dish up with an attractive garnish and place a pat of savoury butter in the centre. This gives a moistness and a touch of luxury to dishes that are otherwise dry and crisp.
For a special soup, too, savoury butters add the finishing touch. Drop a small pat into each bowl just before serving and your guests will have a rich and delicate flavour added to their soup.

Noisette butter

1-2 oz butter
juice of $\frac{1}{2}$ lemon

Method
Melt the butter in a pan and, when brown, add the lemon juice. Use while still foaming.

Parsley butter

$\frac{1}{2}$ oz butter
1 teaspoon chopped parsley
dash of Worcestershire sauce, or
squeeze of lemon juice

Method
Melt butter and when light brown, add parsley and Worcestershire sauce (or lemon juice) and pour over the meat.

Pimiento butter

1 cap canned pimiento
3 oz butter
salt and pepper
cayenne pepper
1 tablespoon double cream
squeeze of lemon juice

Method
Cut the pimiento into small pieces and pound with the other ingredients, seasoning very lightly with cayenne. Press through a sieve and form into pats. Chill and serve with grilled steaks and cutlets.

To make butter pats : pat butter mixture into balls with butter 'hands' (wooden shaping boards), or spread $\frac{1}{4}$-$\frac{1}{2}$ inch thick on greaseproof paper and chill. Cut into small rounds or squares before using.

Maître d'hôtel butter

2 oz unsalted butter
1 dessertspoon chopped parsley
few drops of lemon juice
salt and pepper

Method
Soften the butter on a plate with a palette knife, then add parsley, lemon juice and seasoning to taste.
Serve chilled, in pats, with steaks, mixed grills and fish.

Orange butter

2 oz unsalted butter
grated rind of $\frac{1}{2}$ an orange and 1
teaspoon juice
1 teaspoon tomato purée
salt and pepper

Method
Soften the butter on a plate with a palette knife, and then add other ingredients, seasoning to taste.
Serve chilled, in pats, with lamb cutlets, steaks and fish.

Chutney, garlic, mustard or tomato butters

Other savoury butters are made in the same way using 2 oz unsalted butter with either pounded chutney, crushed garlic, 1 dessertspoon French mustard, or tomato purée.

Anchovy butter

1 oz unsalted butter
2-3 anchovy fillets (soaked in
   milk to remove excess salt)
black pepper (ground from mill)
1 teaspoon anchovy essence

Method
Soften butter on a plate with a palette knife, crush or pound the anchovy fillets and add these to the butter and pepper.

Add anchovy essence to strengthen the flavour and give a delicate pink colour.

Pounding the anchovy fillets before adding them to the butter

Anchovy butter
sauce (for fried steak)

A delicious sauce for fried steak can be made using anchovy butter as the basis. Fry the steak in butter, then add a finely chopped shallot to the pan, lower the heat and cook 2-3 minutes. Pour on 1 wineglass dry white wine and cook until it is reduced to half the quantity. Stir in the anchovy butter and simmer for 2-3 more minutes. Pour the sauce over the steaks.

Sweet sauces

Sweet sauces are the simplest of all to make. Take care when preparing a custard sauce that you don't curdle the mixture, but for the rest you can hardly go wrong. A sadly neglected form of cookery in British homes, sweet sauces go far towards making a simple pudding into the most delicious of desserts.
But remember, you need only small helpings, otherwise the flavour of the dish will be obliterated.

Custard sauce (Crème à la vanille)

½ pint creamy milk
2 tablespoons caster sugar
2-3 drops of vanilla essence, or
½ vanilla pod (split)
2 egg yolks

Method

Put the milk in a pan, add the sugar with vanilla essence or, if using a vanilla pod, infuse it in milk for 10 minutes, keeping pan covered. Take out pod, then add sugar.

Cream the yolks in a bowl, bring the milk to scalding point and pour on gradually. Blend and return to the pan; stir continually over gentle heat with a wooden spatula or spoon. Stir gently to avoid splashing. When the custard coats the spoon and looks creamy, strain back into the bowl.

Dredge a little caster sugar over the top and leave to cool. This coating of sugar melts and helps prevent a skin forming.

Watchpoint Should the custard get too hot and begin to curdle, turn at once into the basin without straining and whisk briskly for 2-3 seconds. Remember that gentle heat helps to prevent a custard from curdling and makes it creamier.

1 *Tipping the infused milk, while still hot, on to thickly creamed egg yolks and sugar*

2 *Testing the consistency of the custard mixture*

Crème caramel
with strawberry sauce

6 oz lump, or granulated, sugar
$\frac{1}{4}$ pint water
1 pint milk
1 tablespoon granulated sugar
2 eggs
2 egg yolks

6-inch diameter charlotte tin (1$\frac{1}{2}$ pints capacity), or No. 2 size soufflé dish

Method
Put the 6 oz sugar and half the water in a heavy pan and dissolve over gentle heat, then boil it steadily to a rich brown caramel. Pour in the remaining water (taking care to cover your hand against any splashes) and stir carefully until all the caramel is dissolved ; then pour it into a bowl to cool. Set oven at 375°F or Mark 5.

Warm the milk with 1 tablespoon sugar and stir until it is dissolved. Break the eggs and yolks with a fork ; do not whisk or make them frothy but just beat them enough to make them smooth. Pour on the warm milk, then stir in the caramel. Strain this mixture into the lightly oiled tin or dish and cover with foil or greaseproof paper. Cook custard au bain-marie in pre-set oven for about 45 minutes until set.

Meanwhile prepare the strawberry sauce (see right).

Allow the custard to stand for about 30 minutes before turning it on to a serving dish. Pour the strawberry sauce around when the custard is completely cool.

Strawberry sauce

$\frac{1}{2}$ lb strawberries
2-3 tablespoons caster, or icing, sugar

Method
Hull and slice the strawberries, dust with some caster (or icing) sugar and leave for 30 minutes. Rub the fruit through a nylon strainer and sweeten with the remaining sugar.

Slicing the strawberries to make the purée for the sauce

Pouring cool caramel into warm custard mixture for crème caramel

Ready to serve, crème caramel with strawberry sauce

Choux pralinés with cherry sauce

choux pastry (see right)
1 tablespoon almonds (blanched
   and finely chopped)
½ pint double cream
1 teaspoon caster sugar
icing sugar (for dredging)

For praline
2 oz almonds (unblanched)
2 oz caster sugar

Some of the ingredients for making
choux pralinés with cherry sauce

Method
Set oven at 400°F or Mark 6.
First prepare praline. Put almonds and sugar into a small
pan and cook slowly to a nut-
brown. Turn on to a greased tin
and when set grind through a
nut mill or Mouli grater.

Prepare choux pastry but
reserve about 1 teaspoon of
beaten egg. Pipe out into balls
or put out in rounds with a
dessertspoon on a dampened
baking sheet. Brush tops with the
reserved egg and sprinkle with
the chopped almonds. Bake in
the oven on a rising temperature

for about 25 minutes until very firm to the touch. Prick sides to release steam and leave to cool.

Whip cream, sweeten with caster sugar and fold in the praline. Make a small hole in the choux and put the cream in ; dust with icing sugar and put on a serving dish.

Make the sauce and serve separately.

Cherry sauce

1 medium can Morello cherries (pitted)
1 dessertspoon arrowroot
1 wineglass red wine
3 tablespoons redcurrant jelly
grated rind of 1 orange

Method
Drain juice from cherries, blend in the arrowroot, bring to the boil in a pan and allow to cool.

Boil the wine in a pan to reduce its quantity by half, add the redcurrant jelly and dissolve it slowly. Add this to the thickened cherry juice, and, when quite cold, stir in the cherries and grated orange rind.

Choux pastry

7½ fl oz water
3 oz butter, or margarine
3¾ oz plain flour
3 eggs

Method
Put water and fat into a fairly large pan. Sift flour on to a piece of paper. Bring contents of the pan to the boil and when bubbling draw pan aside ; allow bubbles to subside and pour in all the flour at once. Stir vigorously until it is smooth (a few seconds).

Cool mixture for about 5 minutes, then beat in the eggs one at a time. If eggs are large, break the last one into a bowl and beat with a fork. Add this slowly to ensure that the mixture remains firm and keeps its shape (you may not need to use all of this last egg).

Beat pastry for about 3 minutes until it looks glossy. It is then ready to be piped out, with a plain éclair pipe.

Choux pastry should be baked in a hot oven on a rising temperature, ie. cooked for 10 minutes at 400°F or Mark 6, then the cooking completed at 425°F or Mark 7, for the length of time given in the recipe.

Chocolate puddings with chocolate sauce

3 oz plain block chocolate
$\frac{1}{4}$ pint milk
5 oz stale cake crumbs
2 oz butter
2 rounded tablespoons caster sugar
2 large eggs (separated)
2-3 drops of vanilla essence

8 castle pudding tins (small moulds)

Method

Cut up the chocolate, melt it slowly in the milk in a saucepan, then bring to the boil and pour over the cake crumbs in a basin. Mix well with a fork, cover and leave for 20-30 minutes.

Have ready a steamer over a pan of boiling water.

Soften the butter in a bowl, add the sugar and work until mixture is light. Beat in the egg yolks and then add the soaked crumbs and vanilla. Whisk the egg whites until stiff and use a metal spoon to fold them carefully into the mixture.

Divide mixture into the buttered pudding tins, cover with foil, or with a piece of buttered greaseproof paper, tie down securely and steam until set (45-50 minutes). Turn on to a hot dish, dust with caster sugar and serve with hot chocolate sauce.

Chocolate sauce

1 tablespoon cocoa
2 tablespoons granulated sugar
$\frac{1}{2}$ pint water
2-3 drops of vanilla essence

Method

Put the cocoa and sugar in a deep saucepan, mix smoothly with the water and then bring slowly to the boil, stirring from time to time. Simmer gently for 10 minutes, add the vanilla essence and serve.

Eve's pudding
with rich orange cream sauce

3 large cooking apples
2 tablespoons granulated sugar
grated rind and juice of ½ lemon
1 tablespoon water
3 oz butter
3 oz caster sugar
1 large egg
5 oz self-raising flour
pinch of salt
2-3 tablespoons milk

6-inch diameter pie dish

Method

Peel and core the apples, cut in thick slices and put in a pan with granulated sugar, lemon juice and water ; cook until apple is tender. Place at the bottom of a pie dish. Set oven at 375°F or Mark 5.

Soften the butter with the lemon rind in a bowl, add the caster sugar and work until light and fluffy. Beat in the egg and then with a metal spoon fold in the flour sifted with the salt. Stir in enough milk to give a dropping consistency.

Spread the mixture over the apple and bake for about 40 minutes in pre-set oven. Serve hot with the sauce.

Rich orange cream sauce

grated rind and juice of 3
    oranges (to give ¼ pint)
juice of 1 lemon
4 oz granulated sugar
2 oz unsalted butter
2 eggs (well beaten)
3-4 fl oz double cream
    (lightly whipped)

Method

Put all the ingredients (except the cream) in a pudding basin. Stand the basin in a pan of boiling water (or use a double boiler), then stir the mixture gently over a low heat until it is thick. Remove from heat.

Watchpoint Do not let the sauce get too hot, otherwise it will curdle.

When the sauce is quite cold fold in the cream.

Banana coconut rolls

6 bananas (peeled)
1 oz butter (melted)
juice of 1 lemon
$\frac{1}{2}$ cup shredded coconut

Method

Set oven at 375°F or Mark 5.

Brush peeled bananas (use ones that are firm and not over-ripe) with melted butter and sprinkle them with lemon juice. Cut them in half crosswise and place in a well-buttered oven-proof dish. Sprinkle well with the coconut.

Bake in the pre-set oven for 15-20 minutes until the bananas are tender and the coconut is browned. Serve hot or cold with rum or pineapple sauce.

Rum sauce

Dissolve 4 oz granulated sugar in $\frac{1}{2}$ cup hot water ; when sugar is completely dissolved, bring to the boil and boil for 5 minutes. Add dark Jamaica rum (you can buy miniature bottles) to taste, with 1 teaspoon lemon juice. (Fresh lime juice is even better than lemon juice, if available.)

Pineapple sauce

Mix together 3 dessertspoons caster sugar, 1 dessertspoon cornflour and a pinch of salt. Add $\frac{3}{4}$ cup unsweetened pine-apple juice and cook the mixture for 5 minutes. Add 1 teaspoon lemon juice and a teacupful of fresh, or canned, crushed pine-apple.

Pears belle Hélène

4-5 even-size pears
syrup (made with 1 pint water
    and 4 oz sugar)
1 vanilla pod (split)

Method

Have the syrup ready in a shallow pan. Peel the pears and carefully core them from the flower end. Lift them into the syrup, add vanilla pod, cover pan and poach gently for 20-30 minutes until tender. Cool in the syrup.

Prepare the Suchard sauce (see below).

To serve, drain the pears thoroughly, dish them up and coat with the Suchard sauce.

Suchard sauce

6 oz plain block chocolate
4 lumps of sugar
1 orange
$\frac{1}{2}$ pint water
3 oz granulated sugar

Method

Rub the sugar lumps over the orange until they are well soaked with the oil from the zest. Break up the chocolate and add it to the water in a pan. Simmer until chocolate is dissolved, then add the granulated sugar ; simmer with pan uncovered until the sauce is syrupy and will coat the back of the spoon. Draw pan aside, add the sugar lumps, stir and reboil ; pour sauce off to cool.

Riz à l'impératrice
with apricot or redcurrant sauce

$3\frac{1}{2}$ oz thick grain rice
$\frac{3}{4}$ pint milk
drop of vanilla essence
2 oz caster sugar
scant 1 oz butter
4 oz glacé fruits
2 tablespoons kirsch
$\frac{1}{2}$ pint double cream

For crème anglaise
4 egg yolks
2 oz caster sugar
scant 8 fl oz milk
scant $\frac{1}{2}$ oz gelatine (softened in
  1 tablespoon water)

Decorative mould (2 pints capacity)

Method

Lightly grease the mould.

Put the rice into cold water, bring to the boil and cook for 2 minutes. Drain well, and return to the pan with the milk and vanilla and cook at a gentle heat, stirring occasionally to prevent sticking, until the rice is tender and the milk absorbed. Add the sugar and butter.

Meanwhile, prepare the crème anglaise ; cream the yolks in a bowl with the sugar, bring the milk to scalding point and pour it over the yolks, then add the gelatine. Stir until gelatine is dissolved and strain.

Cut the fruits into small dice and macerate in the kirsch. When the rice is cold add the custard. Lightly whip the cream and fold into the rice mixture with the glacé fruits, then turn it into lightly greased decorative mould, cover and set on ice or put in the refrigerator to set. For serving, turn it on to a cold plate and pour round the apricot or redcurrant sauce.

Apricot sauce

Soak about $\frac{1}{4}$ lb dried apricots in twice their volume of water overnight, then simmer until tender in the same water with a strip of lemon rind. Rub the apricots through a sieve, sweeten to taste, thin with a little water if necessary and flavour with kirsch.

Redcurrant sauce

Crush $\frac{1}{2}$ lb redcurrants with a fork, then rub through a nylon sieve. Sweeten well with icing sugar and, if too thick, dilute with a light sugar syrup or water. Add kirsch to taste. The sauce should pour easily and must be chilled before serving.

Apple chartreuse with rum and apricot sauce, or soured cream sauce

1 large cooking apple
½ pint water
8 oz lump sugar
pared rind and strained juice of
  1 lemon
2 lb crisp dessert apples (Cox's
  Orange Pippin, or Russet, or
  Sturmer)
4 oz candied fruit (mixture of
  glacé cherry, angelica, pineapple,
  apricot and orange peel)
  — chopped

*6-inch diameter cake tin (1½ pints
capacity), or 6-inch diameter top
(No. 2 size) soufflé dish*

Method

Wipe the cooking apple, remove the stalk and eye, cut in slices but do not remove the peel, core or pips. Put slices in a saucepan with the water, cover and simmer gently until pulpy. Tip into a nylon strainer, over a bowl, and leave undisturbed until all the juice has dripped through. Measure the amount of juice (you need 7½ fl oz) and put this in a large shallow pan with the sugar, rind and lemon juice and set on a low heat. When all the sugar has dissolved, boil juice steadily for 5 minutes, draw pan aside and remove the lemon rind.

Peel and core the dessert apples and slice straight into the pan of juice — they must be cut very evenly and quite thinly (⅛ inch). Cover the pan and cook apples gently for 10-12 minutes. **Watchpoint** During this cooking time turn the apple slices once or twice, taking great care not to break them or let the syrup boil — it should just simmer very gently.

Take the lid off the pan and continue cooking until there is just enough syrup to moisten the apple slices. Draw off the heat, add the candied fruits, cover the pan and leave until the apples look clear. Tip into the wet cake tin or soufflé dish and leave in a cool place to set. (No gelatine is needed with this chartreuse as the natural pectin in the fruit is sufficient to set it.)

Turn chartreuse out of the tin or dish and serve with soured cream sauce, or a sharp rum and apricot sauce. We think the slightly sharp flavour of soured cream goes particularly well here.

Rum and apricot sauce

4 tablespoons smooth apricot jam
2 tablespoons water
juice of ½ lemon
1 tablespoon rum

Method

Put jam, water and the lemon juice in a pan and heat gently to melt the jam. Bring sauce to the boil. Remove from the heat, add rum and strain sauce into a bowl. Serve cold.

Soured cream sauce

Take ¼ pint fresh double cream, whip it until it begins to thicken, then stir in ¼ pint of soured cream and 1 teaspoon caster sugar.

1 The dessert apples are sliced into the saucepan of apple syrup
2 Tipping cooked apples and candied fruits into a soufflé dish to set

Pêches Melba

4 ripe peaches
4 tablespoons granulated sugar
½ pint water
½ vanilla pod
1 pint vanilla ice cream
3-4 fl oz Chantilly cream

4 coupe glasses

Method

Prepare a syrup with the sugar, water and vanilla pod. Peel and halve the peaches, remove stones and put the peaches, rounded side down, in the syrup to poach. (This will take at least 10 minutes.)

Watchpoint The peaches must be ripe. To test if a yellow clingstone peach is ripe, rub the skin gently with the blade of a table knife ; if the fruit is ripe, the skin will peel off very easily. If it doesn't, do not scald the peaches, but simply cut them in half and poach with the skin on. When the fruit is cooked the skin will be easy to peel off.

Allow the peaches to cool in the syrup, then drain. Prepare the Melba sauce.

Just before serving, place a scoop of vanilla ice cream in each coupe glass, arrange two peach halves over it, coat with a tablespoon of Melba sauce and decorate with a rosette of Chantilly cream.

Melba sauce

8 oz fresh, or frozen, raspberries
4-5 tablespoons sifted icing sugar

Method

Rub the raspberries through a nylon strainer and beat the icing sugar into this purée a little at a time until the mixture thickens. Chill.

Pêches Melba, a delicious concoction of ice cream, peaches and raspberries, was created in honour of the opera singer Nellie Melba

Brown bread cream with damson sauce

3 slices wholemeal bread (2-3 days old)
1 tablespoon caster sugar
$\frac{3}{4}$ pint milk
pared rind and juice of $\frac{1}{2}$ lemon
3 egg yolks
$1\frac{1}{2}$ oz caster sugar
5 tablespoons water
$\frac{1}{2}$ oz gelatine
$\frac{1}{4}$ pint double cream

Decorative mould, or glass bowl ($1\frac{1}{4}$-$1\frac{1}{2}$ pints capacity)

Method

Remove the crusts from the bread and rub through a wire sieve or reduce to crumbs a little at a time in a liquidiser. Set the oven at 350°F or Mark 4. Spread out the crumbs on a sheet of greaseproof paper on a baking sheet, dust with 1 tablespoon sugar and put in the preset oven to brown. Allow to cool.
Watchpoint Great care must be taken to brown the crumbs as evenly as possible, so turn them with a fork several times while they are browning. The time the crumbs take to brown will depend on the freshness of the bread, but allow 10 minutes — they must be very crisp.

Heat the milk with the lemon rind to scalding point, cover and leave to infuse. Lightly oil the mould, or have ready the glass bowl. Work the egg yolks and sugar together with a wooden spoon until thick and light in colour, strain on the hot milk. Pour the water and lemon juice on to the gelatine and leave soaking. Return the egg and milk mixture to the rinsed saucepan and stir briskly over heat until it thickens and coats the back of the wooden spoon. Strain quickly into a large bowl, add the soaked gelatine, stir until dissolved and then leave to cool, but not in a refrigerator.

When the custard is quite cold, tip it into a thin saucepan. Lightly whip the cream and fold it into the custard. Stand the saucepan in a bowl of cold water with a few ice cubes added. Stir gently until the custard is on the point of setting, then quickly fold in the crisp brown breadcrumbs. Pour it into the prepared mould or glass bowl, cover and leave in the refrigerator, or in a cool place, for 1-2 hours to set. Meanwhile make the damson sauce (see opposite).

To serve, turn the cream out of the mould and pour the sauce over or around it. Or, if the cream is served from the glass bowl, decorate with a little extra cream and hand the sauce separately.

Crumbs made from slices of stale wholemeal bread are dusted with sugar, then browned in the oven

Damson sauce

½ lb damsons
½ pint water
4 tablespoons granulated sugar

Method

Cook the damsons with the water and sugar until soft and pulpy, then rub through a strainer. (Damson jelly or home-made damson cheese can also be used ; just melt it in a saucepan over heat with 2-3 tablespoons of water, then cool.)

The pan of custard is placed in a bowl of cold water and ice cubes to speed setting. When it is about to set, the browned crumbs are quickly folded in

The brown bread cream is set in a decorative mould and the damson sauce is poured over it. Alternatively serve the cream in a glass bowl and hand the sauce separately

Castle puddings with banana sauce

or apricot jam, red jam or marmalade sauce

4 oz butter
4 oz caster sugar
2 eggs
2-3 drops of vanilla essence
4 oz self-raising flour
pinch of salt

Dariole moulds

Method
Grease the moulds well and have ready a steamer on a pan full of boiling water.

Soften the butter in a bowl, add the sugar and work until soft and light. Beat in the eggs a little at a time, add the vanilla essence, then fold in sifted flour and salt with a metal spoon.

Turn the mixture into the moulds, cover with pleated buttered greaseproof paper and foil (make a 1-inch pleat to allow pudding to rise) and tie down with string. Steam for 45-50 minutes. Turn on to a hot dish and spoon round the hot sauce.

Watchpoint The moulds should be only three-parts full to allow the pudding to rise.

Banana sauce on castle puddings

Banana sauce

1 banana (finely sliced)
juice of $\frac{1}{2}$ lemon (made up to
    8 fl oz with water)
1 tablespoon maraschino, or juice
    from maraschino cherries
1 oz granulated sugar
1 dessertspoon arrowroot

Method
Put the lemon juice, water and maraschino or juice into a pan with the sugar and dissolve over gentle heat. Mix the arrowroot smoothly with 1 tablespoon water, stir into the pan and boil until clear. Add the sliced banana and serve hot.

Apricot jam, red jam, or marmalade, sauce

2 rounded tablespoons of home-
    made apricot, or red, jam, or
    marmalade
about $7\frac{1}{2}$ fl oz water
2 strips of lemon rind (if using
    apricot jam, or marmalade)
1 tablespoon granulated sugar
1 tablespoon arrowroot (slaked with
    1 tablespoon water) — optional

Method
Put all the ingredients, except the arrowroot, into a pan and bring slowly to the boil, stirring well. Taste, and if not strong enough in flavour add a little more jam or marmalade. Continue to simmer for 5-6 minutes, then remove the lemon rind and thicken if necessary with the arrowroot. Serve hot.

Baked vanilla soufflé with red wine sauce

1 vanilla pod, or $\frac{1}{2}$ teaspoon vanilla
   essence
$\frac{1}{2}$ pint milk
2 rounded tablespoons caster sugar
1 tablespoon plain flour
1 dessertspoon arrowroot
1 oz butter
3 egg yolks
4 egg whites
little sifted icing sugar

7-inch diameter top (No. 1 size)
soufflé dish

Method

Reserve 4 tablespoons of the milk. If using vanilla pod, infuse it in the remaining milk. Tie a band of greaseproof paper round the soufflé dish so that it extends by 3 inches above top. Grease dish and paper rim. Set oven at 375°F or Mark 5.

Bring the milk to the boil, add the sugar and vanilla essence (if using), cover and draw aside. Blend the reserved milk with the flour and arrowroot, add to the pan of milk, return to the heat and stir until boiling. Boil for 2-3 seconds, then draw aside, dot with the butter, cover and leave for 5 minutes. Then stir to mix in butter, and beat in yolks one at a time. Whip whites to a firm snow, and cut and fold into the mixture.

Turn into the soufflé dish and bake in pre-set oven for 20 minutes. Dust the top with icing sugar and put back in the oven for 4-5 minutes to caramelise the top.

Red wine sauce

1 tablespoon granulated sugar
$\frac{1}{4}$ pint water
2 tablespoons red jam
rind of $\frac{1}{4}$ lemon
1 teaspoon arrowroot (slaked
   with 1 tablespoon water)
2 tablespoons claret

Method

Place the sugar, water, jam and lemon rind in the pan and slowly bring to the boil. Simmer gently for about 8 minutes, then thicken with the slaked arrowroot. Cook until clear, add the wine, strain and serve hot.

Brandy butter

(Senior Wrangler sauce)

4 oz unsalted butter
4 oz caster sugar
2-3 tablespoons brandy (to taste)

This butter is good with plum pudding and mince pies.

Method

Cream the butter thoroughly, beat in the sugar by degrees and continue to beat until white. Then beat in the brandy, a teaspoon at a time. Pile up in a small dish or bowl and chill until firm.

Senior Wrangler is a title dating from 1750, given to Cambridge undergraduates who passed first class in their Mathematics Tripos. The name was given to brandy butter by a forebear of Rosemary Hume, Dr. Whewell, who was a Second Wrangler and Master of Trinity in the mid-19th century.

Rum butter

3 oz unsalted butter
3 oz soft brown sugar
grated rind of $\frac{1}{2}$ lemon and
squeeze of juice
2-3 tablespoons rum

This hard sauce is excellent with plum pudding and mince pies. In Cumberland it is served at christening parties. A small pinch each of cinnamon and nutmeg may be substituted for the lemon juice and rind.

Method

Cream the butter thoroughly, then add the sugar gradually with the lemon rind and juice. Continue to beat, adding the rum gradually to flavour the butter well. Pile up in a small dish and chill before serving.

Lemon butter

3 oz unsalted butter
grated rind of 1 lemon
2 oz caster, or icing, sugar
juice of $\frac{1}{2}$ lemon

Serve with pancakes and steamed puddings.

Method

Soften the butter in a bowl with the grated rind of the lemon. Add the caster or icing sugar a little at a time with the lemon juice and beat mixture until light and fluffy. Pile into a small dish and leave until very firm before serving.

Sweet mousseline sauce

1 egg
1 egg yolk
1½ oz caster sugar
2 tablespoons sherry, or fruit
   juice

Serve with steamed, or baked sponge, puddings.

Method
Put all the ingredients together in a bowl. Whisk over a pan of simmering water until mixture is thick and frothy.
Watchpoint Use as soon as possible, but if it has to be kept a little while, whisk it for a minute before serving.

Hot sabayon sauce

3 egg yolks
1 tablespoon caster sugar
¼ pint sherry
small strip of lemon rind

Serve with fruit puddings.

Method
Put all the ingredients into a small basin and stand it over a small pan, one-quarter filled with simmering water. Whisk the sauce until it becomes very frothy and starts to thicken. Remove the lemon rind and serve at once.

Cold sabayon sauce

2 oz granulated sugar
2½ fl oz water
2 egg yolks
grated rind and juice of ½
   lemon
1 tablespoon rum, or brandy, or
   2 tablespoons golden sherry
¼ pint double cream

Serve over fresh or sugared fruit, apple charlotte and other fruit puddings.

Method
Dissolve the sugar gently in the water, then boil until the syrup will form a thread between your finger and thumb. Put the egg yolks into a bowl and beat well. Take the syrup off the heat, allow the bubbles to subside and pour on to the yolks, whisking well. Whisk the mixture until thick, add the grated lemon rind and juice.

Flavour with the rum, brandy or sherry and continue to whisk for 1-2 minutes. Whisk the cream until it will just hold its shape, fold it into sauce and chill.

Fudge sauce

3 oz soft light brown sugar
1 tablespoon golden syrup
½ pint milk
2 oz butter
½ vanilla pod (split)
2 teaspoons (arrowroot slaked
   with 1 tablespoon water)

Serve hot with coffee parfait, vanilla or coffee ice cream, or steamed ginger or coffee pudding.

Hot fudge sauce is good poured over coffee ice cream

Method
Put the sugar and syrup in a heavy pan and dissolve over gentle heat. In another saucepan heat the milk with the butter and vanilla, and leave it to infuse.

After about 10 minutes, when milk is well flavoured with vanilla, remove the pod from pan. Boil the sugar mixture until caramelised, then add the milk mixture, stirring until the lumps are dissolved, beat until smooth. Add slaked arrowroot, and boil for 1 minute. Serve at once.

Butterscotch sauce

1 tablespoon golden syrup
½ oz butter
2 tablespoons demerara sugar
½ pint warm water
squeeze of lemon juice
1 dessertspoon custard powder
  (slaked with 1 tablespoon water)

Serve with ice cream.

Method
Put the syrup, butter and sugar into a pan and cook to a rich brown toffee. Draw aside, add the warm water carefully and then lemon juice. Boil up sauce and pour on to slaked custard powder — reboil to thicken and cook custard.

Caramel sauce

6 oz granulated sugar
2½ fl oz cold water
¼ pint warm water

Serve either plain or with one sliced banana added to it, with a squeeze of lemon juice also added just before serving. It is also good served with little choux filled with cream, or vanilla bavarois.

Method
Dissolve the sugar slowly in the cold water, then boil rapidly until a good caramel. Draw aside, add the warm water carefully then stir over heat until dissolved, then boil rapidly until syrupy, ie. the consistency of thin cream. Pour off and cool. If it thickens too much on cooling add 1-2 tablespoons warm water. Serve when cold.

Walnut and apple sauce

1 oz walnut kernels (coarsely chopped)
1 lb cooking apples
$\frac{1}{2}$ oz butter
pared rind of $\frac{1}{2}$ lemon
3 oz granulated sugar
$\frac{1}{2}$ cup water

This is served with either ice cream, caramel bavarois or rice pudding.

Method

Rub the butter round a sauté pan. Wipe the apples, quarter, core and slice into the pan. Add lemon rind, cover apples with a piece of foil or greaseproof paper and then put on lid and cook over gentle heat to a pulp. Rub through a strainer.

Rinse out the pan, dissolve sugar in the water over gentle heat, then boil for about 3-4 minutes, until it is a thick syrup. Draw pan aside and stir in the apple pulp. Return the pan to the heat and simmer the mixture until it is the consistency of cream.

Add the walnuts to the sauce. Cook for 1 minute then draw aside. Serve hot or cold.

Orange cream sauce

1 large, or 2 small, oranges
5 lumps of sugar
$\frac{1}{4}$ pint double cream (lightly whipped)

For custard
$\frac{1}{4}$ pint milk
1 teaspoon caster sugar
2 egg yolks (mixed with 1 teaspoon arrowroot)

Serve with ice cream, cold sweets and steamed or baked puddings.

Method

Cream the egg yolks with the sugar. Heat the milk to scalding point and pour it slowly on to the yolks. Blend and return to the pan ; stir over gentle heat until custard coats the back of the spoon. Leave to get cold.

Thinly pare rind from half the orange with a potato peeler, cut into fine shreds and simmer until tender. Drain well and set them aside for decoration.

Rub the lump sugar over the second half of orange to remove all the zest — each lump should be completely saturated with the oil from the skin. Place these lumps in a small basin, strain the juice from the oranges and pour 5 tablespoons of this juice over the sugar lumps, stir until the sugar is dissolved. Stir the orange syrup into the cream and the cold custard, together with fine shreds of orange rind.

Salad dressings

Summer and winter salads, all need a light dressing to make the best of them. You will need only a little at a time, but make enough to store. Keep in a screw-top bottle in the refrigerator and you will never be at a loss for something to liven up an otherwise ordinary dish.

French dressing

1 tablespoon vinegar (red or
　white wine, or tarragon)
$\frac{1}{2}$ teaspoon salt
$\frac{1}{2}$ teaspoon black pepper (ground
　from mill)
fresh herbs (chopped — thyme,
　marjoram, basil or parsley) —
　optional
3 tablespoons olive oil, or
　groundnut oil

True French dressing does not
have sugar, but for English
tastes add a good pinch. When
herbs are added to French
dressing it is called vinaigrette.

Method
Mix vinegar with the seasonings, add oil and when the
dressing thickens, taste for correct seasoning. More salt should
be added if the dressing is sharp
yet oily. Quantities should be in
the ratio of 1 part vinegar to 3
parts oil.

Roquefort dressing

2 oz Roquefort cheese
1 teaspoon Worcestershire sauce
2 tablespoons double cream
4-5 tablespoons French dressing
$\frac{1}{2}$ teaspoon finely grated onion

Method
First prepare the dressing.
Work the Roquefort until quite
smooth, adding the Worcestershire sauce and cream, then
gradually add the French dressing
and finely grated onion.

Alabama sauce

1 red, or green, pepper
1 clove of garlic (crushed with salt)
2-3 sticks of celery
$\frac{1}{4}$ pint boiled dressing (see below)
2 fl oz double cream
1 teaspoon horseradish cream
2-3 tablespoons tomato chutney
sugar
salt and pepper
dash of Tabasco sauce

Method
Split, seed and chop pepper.
Blanch, refresh and drain. Chop
celery then stir into dressing
with the pepper and remaining
ingredients. Season highly with
sugar, salt and pepper to taste,
and a dash of Tabasco.

This sauce should have the
consistency of mayonnaise.

Boiled dressing

1 tablespoon caster sugar
1 dessertspoon plain flour
1 teaspoon salt
1 dessertspoon made mustard
1 tablespoon water
$\frac{1}{4}$ pint each vinegar and water
　(mixed)
1 egg
$\frac{1}{2}$ oz butter
cream, or creamy milk

Method
Mix dry ingredients together,
add mustard and about 1 tablespoon of water. Add to vinegar
and water and cook thoroughly
for about 5 minutes. Beat egg,
add butter, pour on the hot
vinegar mixture and beat
thoroughly.

When cold, dilute with cream
or milk and mix well. This
dressing keeps well, covered,
in a refrigerator.

Scandinavian dressing

1 dessertspoon caraway, or dill
  seeds (crushed)
$\frac{1}{4}$ pint water (boiling)
1 teaspoon salt
1$\frac{1}{2}$ tablespoons vinegar
2 teaspoons caster sugar

Method

Make caraway liquid by crushing 1 dessertspoon caraway seeds (or dill) and scald with $\frac{1}{4}$ pint boiling water. Cool and strain. Reserve 2 tablespoons of caraway liquid and store remaining liquid in a screw-top jar for future use. It will keep up to 2 weeks in a cool place.

Add other ingredients to caraway liquid and mix all together. This dressing is good with a plain beetroot side salad.

Tarragon cream dressing

1 egg
2 oz caster sugar
3 tablespoons tarragon vinegar
salt and pepper
$\frac{1}{4}$ pint double cream

Method

Break egg into a bowl and beat with a fork. Add sugar and gradually add vinegar. Stand bowl in a pan of boiling water, stir mixture until beginning to thicken, then draw off heat and continue to stir. When mixture has the consistency of thick cream, take basin out of pan, stir for a few seconds longer, season lightly and leave till cold.

Partially whip cream and fold into the dressing.

This dressing can be made up (without cream) in large quantities and stored, when cold, in a screw-top jar in the refrigerator. It will keep for 2-3 weeks. When needed, take out required amount and add cream.

Mayonnaise

2 egg yolks
salt and pepper
dry mustard
$\frac{3}{4}$ cup of salad oil
2 tablespoons wine vinegar

This recipe makes $\frac{1}{2}$ pint. Eggs should not come straight from the refrigerator. If oil is cloudy or chilled, warm it by putting bottle in a pan of hot water for a short time.

Method

Work egg yolks and seasonings with a small whisk or wooden spoon in a bowl until thick ; then start adding the oil drop by drop. This must be done very carefully to prevent mayonnaise curdling. When 2 tablespoons of oil have been added this mixture will be very thick. Now carefully stir in 1 teaspoon of the vinegar.

The remaining oil can then be added a little more quickly, either 1 tablespoon at a time and beaten thoroughly between each addition until it is absorbed, or in a thin steady stream if you are using an electric beater. When all the oil has been absorbed, add remaining vinegar to taste, and extra salt and pepper as necessary.

To thin and lighten mayonnaise add a little hot water. For a coating consistency, thin with a little cream or milk.

Note : if mayonnaise curdles, start with a fresh yolk in another bowl and work well with seasoning, then add the curdled mixture to it very slowly and carefully. When curdled mixture is completely incorporated, more oil can be added if the mixture is too thin.

Lemon cream dressing

$\frac{1}{4}$ pint mayonnaise
$\frac{1}{4}$ pint cream (lightly whipped)
grated rind and juice of $\frac{1}{2}$ lemon
salt and pepper
made mustard

Method

Stir the cream into the mayonnaise, adding the grated rind and lemon juice gradually. Season well ; add mustard to taste. Add 1 tablespoon of boiling water, if necessary, as the dressing should be thin. (It can be made with less cream and more mayonnaise.)

Cauliflower with mustard mayonnaise

1 large cauliflower
1 carrot (grated)
$\frac{1}{2}$ pint mayonnaise
1 rounded teaspoon French mustard
salt and pepper
little creamy milk, or single cream (optional)
paprika pepper

Method

Wash cauliflower, break into sprigs and cook in boiling, salted water until barely tender (about 10 minutes). Drain and refresh. Dry sprigs thoroughly in absorbent paper or cloth, arrange in salad dish or bowl.

Grate carrot finely and fold into mayonnaise with mustard. If too thick, dilute with a little milk or cream. Spoon mayonnaise over cauliflower and dust with paprika pepper.

Mayonnaise Nantua

3 oz shrimps, or prawns (with shells)
½ pint olive oil
½ teaspoon paprika pepper
2-3 egg yolks
salt and pepper
about 1½-2 dessertspoons white wine vinegar (to taste)

Serve with a cold fish such as salmon or sea trout.

Method
Shell the shrimps (or the prawns). Peel the body shell away where it joins the head, then give the tail a firm pinch and draw it gently off the meat. Pound the shells with the paprika in the oil and leave to soak for 10-15 minutes. Chop the prawns roughly, or leave shrimps whole, and strain the oil.

To make mayonnaise : work egg yolks and seasonings with a small whisk or wooden spoon in a bowl until thick ; then start adding the strained oil drop by drop (when 2 tablespoons of oil have been added, the mixture will be very thick). Now carefully stir in 1 teaspoon of the vinegar. Add the remaining oil more quickly ; either 1 tablespoon at a time and beaten thoroughly between each addition until it is absorbed, or, if you are using an electric beater, in a thin, steady stream.

When all the oil is absorbed, add remaining vinegar to taste, extra seasoning, if necessary, and the shrimps (or prawns).

Prawns sicilienne

6 oz rice (boiled)
French dressing (to moisten) — see page 93
paprika pepper
1½ oz almonds (blanched and shredded)
salt and pepper

6-8 dariole moulds

Method
Mix the rice with French dressing (coloured with the paprika) and add the almonds. Season well. Put into the dariole moulds and set aside.

Prepare the sauce (see below). Turn out the moulds and spoon the sauce round the rice.

Watchpoint Soak almonds (either before or after splitting and shredding) in warm water for 30 minutes or longer. This makes them juicy and tender and like a fresh nut. Drain well and dry before adding to rice.

Sicilienne mayonnaise

¼ pint thick mayonnaise (see page 95)
juice of 1 orange
juice of ½ lemon
1-2 caps of pimiento (sieved)
1 shallot (finely chopped)
2½ fl oz strong fresh tomato pulp
4 oz prawns (shelled)
salt and pepper

Method
Combine the ingredients in the order given and season to taste.

Eggs mollets à l'indienne

5 eggs
4 oz long grain Patna rice (cooked, drained and dried)
2-3 tablespoons French dressing (see page 93)
salt and pepper

To garnish
pimiento (shredded)
watercress

Method

First prepare the curry mayonnaise (see right).

Softboil or poach the eggs. Moisten the rice with a little French dressing ; arrange down the centre of a serving dish.

Adjust seasoning and spoon curry mayonnaise over the eggs. Garnish with the pimiento and watercress.

Curry mayonnaise

1 shallot (finely chopped)
1 tablespoon oil
1 dessertspoon curry powder
1 teaspoon paprika pepper
1 teaspoon tomato purée (diluted with $\frac{1}{2}$ cup of water), or $\frac{1}{2}$ cup of tomato juice
2 slices of lemon
1 dessertspoon apricot jam
$\frac{1}{2}$ pint thick mayonnaise (see page 95)

Method

Soften the shallot in oil, add curry powder and paprika and after 3-4 seconds the remaining ingredients. Stir well and simmer for 4-5 minutes. Strain and add enough of the curry mixture to the mayonnaise to flavour it well.

Eggs mollets à l'indienne — in a curry mayonnaise, garnished with strips of pimiento and watercress

Prawn cocktail

with tomato mayonnaise

8 oz frozen prawns (allow at
　　least 1½ oz per person)
1 small lettuce (finely shredded)
paprika pepper (for dusting)
4-8 prawns in their shells (for
　　garnish)

For tomato mayonnaise
½ pint thick mayonnaise (see page
　　95)
1 dessertspoon tomato ketchup
salt and pepper
dash of Tabasco sauce
1 large tablespoon double cream
squeeze of lemon juice

Glass goblets for serving

Method

Thaw out prawns thoroughly.
Combine the mayonnaise ingredients. Add about half to the
prawns, just enough to coat
nicely. Put shredded lettuce in
the bottom of the goblets, arrange prawns on top and coat
with rest of sauce. Dust with
paprika and garnish each serving with 1-2 fresh prawns, with
the body and tail shell removed
but the head left on.

Anchovy mayonnaise

2 teaspoons anchovy essence
½ pint mayonnaise (see page 95)
1 tablespoon chopped parsley,
　　or chopped capers
1 tablespoon chopped dill
　　cucumber
1 small clove of garlic (chopped
　　with a good pinch of salt)
3 black olives (stoned and
　　chopped)
1 egg (hard-boiled)
1-2 tablespoons double cream
　　(optional)

Method

Mix the mayonnaise with the
parsley (or capers) and anchovy
essence and dill cucumber. Add
the garlic to the mayonnaise
mixture with the chopped
olives, the egg white (finely
chopped) and the yolk (rubbed
through a wire strainer). Taste
for seasoning and, if a little
sharp, soften with 1-2 tablespoons cream.

Sole éventail with mayonnaise collée

2 soles (1¼ lb each) — filleted
  and skinned
juice of ½ lemon

For farce
12 oz-1 lb whiting (filleted) — to
  give approximately 8 oz
  minced fish
2 egg whites
¼ pint double cream
salt and pepper

For garnish
8 button mushrooms (sliced and
  cooked)
1½-2 pints aspic jelly

Method
Skin and trim the fillets, wash
and dry them well, then bat
them out carefully. Set oven at
325°F or Mark 3.

To prepare farce : gradually
work minced fish with egg
whites, then beat in the cream ;
season and set aside.

Spread farce on the skinned
side of each fillet ; fold over the
tail section and smooth the
sides. Make sure that each fillet
is pointed at the end. Arrange
fillets in a lightly buttered oven-
proof dish, sprinkle with lemon

juice, cover with a piece of foil
or buttered paper and poach in
pre-set oven for 12-15 minutes.
Strain off liquor and leave the
fillets to cool.

Set fillets on a cake rack,
with a large plate or tray under-
neath, and pour over mayonnaise collée (see below). Leave
them for 10-12 minutes, then
garnish with sliced mushrooms.

When set, baste fillets with a
little cool aspic jelly.

Chop the remaining aspic,
arrange it on a silver or stainless
steel dish and place the fillets
on top in the shape of a fan.
Garnish with aspic croûtons.

Mayonnaise collée
½ pint mayonnaise (see page 95)
¼ oz (1 rounded teaspoon)
  gelatine
2½ fl oz aspic jelly

Method
Dissolve gelatine in aspic jelly
and stir into the mayonnaise.
Wait until it is on the point of
setting (as thick as cream)
before coating the fillets.

Salsa verde (Green sauce)

1 large handful of parsley
1 rounded tablespoon capers
1-2 cloves of garlic
1-2 anchovy fillets
3-5 tablespoons olive oil
1 slice of white bread (crust removed)
1 tablespoon lemon juice
salt and pepper

Serve salsa verde with vegetables

Method

Pick the parsley from the stalks, chop it ; pound or blend with capers, garlic and anchovies. Spoon 1-2 tablespoons of oil over the bread and, when soaked, add to the parsley mixture and continue to pound. Gradually add 2-3 tablespoons of oil ; add lemon juice and season well. The sauce should be thick.

Seasonings

Here is the chance to really experiment. Learn all about the herbs and spices you have never used, as well as a few new tips about those you use regularly. As you prepare your family's meals, try the variety you can introduce by using a different seasoning. You will have even more fun out of using herbs if you can grow some of your own. Then you can use them, fresh and dried, at will.
Follow the charts on pages 104 - 107 for what to use with what.

Salt

Salt is a mineral that is used in cooking and preparing food, for seasoning and preserving. The higher the vegetable content of your diet, the greater is the need for salt. There are two main kinds — sea salt and rock salt. **Sea salt** consists of crystals of sodium chloride dried out of sea water. It contains more impurities than refined rock salt. It can be used at table, though it is not fine enough to pour.

Rock salt is obtained by drilling into the earth about 1000 feet, pouring down water and pumping up the resultant brine from the layer of marl below the earth's surface. Unrefined rock salt is greyish in appearance, can be used in a salt mill or grinder and is coarser than table salt.

Table salt is highly refined to remove any impurities, looks fine and white, and has a very small proportion of magnesium carbonate added to it to make it free-running and less likely to clog in damp atmospheres.

Iodised table salt can be bought and is used for medical purposes where there is a deficiency of iodine in a person's diet.

Cooking or kitchen salt is coarser and less expensive than table salt. It is usually sold in bags, but can still be obtained in block form, though this is less pure. Cooking salt should be stored in a dry place in an airtight container as it readily absorbs moisture. When used in preserving it destroys harmful micro-organism.

Freezing salt is simply coarse rock salt. It is added to ice when making cream and water ices because brine freezes at a lower temperature than water.

Pepper

Peppercorns are the dried berries of the plant *Piper nigrum,* native to the East Indies. They are used to flavour stocks, stews, and some savoury sauces, but should always be removed before serving. Black peppercorns have the outer husk still on them ; white peppercorns, milder than the black, have the outer husk removed. Peppercorns may be ground at home in a peppermill.

Ready-ground black or **white pepper** produces a less aromatic and pungent result than whole peppercorns and is better bought only in small quantities, as it loses its flavour much more quickly. White pepper is used when specks of black would spoil the appearance of a dish.

Cayenne pepper is a very hot, pungent spice and should be used sparingly. It is especially good with meat, egg and cheese dishes. Ground from one of the many varieties of the *Capsicum* family, *Capsicum frutescens,* it is native to America but cultivated in most of the warm parts of the world. (**Chilli** powder and **paprika** are ground from varieties of the same family, paprika being prepared from Hungarian or Spanish pepper.)

Jamaican pepper, or allspice, is an aromatic spice made from the berries of a Jamaican evergreen of the myrtle species. The ripe berries resemble peppercorns, but are larger and less pungent in flavour. These are dried and then ground for the preparation of allspice, used in biscuits and cakes (it tastes of a combination of cloves, cinnamon and nutmeg). The whole berries are used for marinades, pickles and savoury dishes.

Herb chart

	BASIL	CHIVES	MARJORAM
SOUPS	Tomato & most others		
FISH	Shrimps, white fish		★
MEAT (roasts & grills)	Lamb, pork, veal	Stuffings	Veal, lamb, pork, sausag
STEWS	Beef		★
POULTRY & GAME			Stuffing for goose
VEGETABLES	Tomatoes, broad beans	Potatoes	Tomatoes
SALADS & SALAD DRESSINGS	Green salad, tomato	★	★
EGG DISHES	Tomato & fines herbes omelets	Omelets	Omelets ★
CHEESE DISHES		Cream cheese	Cream chees pizza
SAUCES	For pastas, rice		
OTHER USES	Tomato dishes		

We have placed a ★ as well as, or instead of, a specific suggestion to indicate the herb /spice goes well with other items within the categories listed.

PARSLEY	ROSEMARY	SAGE	THYME	MIXED HERBS
★	Minestrone ★	Fish chowder	★	
★			Stuffings ★	If cooked à la meunière
Stuffings	Roast lamb ★	Stuffing for pork	Stuffings	Stuffings
			(in bouquet garni) ★	★
Stuffings (with other herbs)		Stuffing for duck, goose, turkey (with other herbs)	Stuffing for rabbit, chicken (with other herbs)	★
Potatoes	Sauté potatoes		Tomatoes	
Chopped with other herbs for salads			Chopped with other herbs for salads	Green salad, vinaigrette ★
Omelets			For stuffing and sprinkling	Omelets ★
		★	Cream cheese ★	★
★				
Maître d'hôtel butter	Herb tea			

Spice chart

	PEPPER (black & white)	CAYENNE	CINNAMON
SOUPS	★		
FISH	★	Shellfish	
MEAT (roasts & grills)	★	★	
STEWS	★		
POULTRY & GAME	★		
VEGETABLES	★		
SALADS & SALAD DRESSINGS	★	Some dressings	
EGG DISHES	★	★	
CHEESE DISHES	★	Welsh rarebit, cheese sablés	
SAUCES	★	Newburg sauce (for lobster)	
OTHER USES			Cakes, pies, toast, mulled wine, pickles etc.

...OVES	CURRY	GINGER	PAPRIKA	MIXED SPICE
	Shellfish ★	★	Shellfish ★	
...am		★	Lamb, pork, veal	
★	★		Hungarian goulash ★	
★	Chicken	Duck	Chicken ★	
	★			
	★		Various Spanish omelet	
...ead sauce	Curry sauces, for shellfish, chicken, eggs		Cream sauces	Bottled sauces
...ttled sauces, ...utney, ...lled wine, ...it cake		Cakes, biscuits, fruit chutney	Rice	Fruit cakes

Herbs

Balm
The aromatic foliage of this perennial plant smells of lemon. It is seldom used in cooking, but a large handful of fresh or dried balm, infused in boiling water, makes a good tisane (tea).

Basil (sweet)
This half-hardy annual is especially good for flavouring tomato dishes. It is spicy and fragrant, with a bright green leaf.

Bay
Together with parsley and thyme, a bayleaf forms the traditional bouquet garni. It has a strong flavour, particularly when fresh, so unless recipes call for more, use only half a bayleaf to flavour soups, meat dishes and sauces. The bay tree is very attractive and can be grown in the garden or in a tub.

Chervil
This annual is frequently coupled with tarragon to add to sauces and dressings. It has a bright green, delicate curly leaf with a pronounced flavour. Chervil has value in soups where, for example, small sprigs are used to garnish a potato soup. It can also be used in omelets and salads.

Chives
This herb is a necessity for every garden and window box. A perennial herb that is used snipped (with scissors) in salads, creamed cheeses or in stuffings when a subtle flavour of onion is called for.

Dill
This annual is by far the best to grow in preference to fennel. It is delicate in flavour, and pretty and feathery in appearance. Dill is the herb to use with fish, either in a sauce or chopped and sprinkled over it. It is more delicate and subtle in flavour than fennel and marries well with cucumber.

The stalks and seeds are used in pickles, eg. cucumber, and the seeds only for flavouring salads and vegetables, especially white cabbage and marrow.

Fennel
A tall and rampant perennial plant which produces more foliage than one can ever use. Strong in taste, it must be used sparingly, eg. in fish sauces.

Florence fennel (finocchio)
These are thick, fleshy white bulbs, crisp and juicy and tasting of aniseed. They are delicious sliced raw in a salad, or quartered, plainly boiled, tossed in butter and served as a special vegetable.

To grow to any size, the bulbs need plenty of sunshine and moisture at the right time, so Florence fennel is imported and appears in the shops in spring and early summer.

Garlic
A bulb similar to an onion but divided into sections called cloves. These are covered with a fine skin which is removed before chopping, crushing or using them whole. For some dishes the 'cloves' are left unpeeled before cooking and taken out before serving (this gives a delicate flavour).

Garlic can be grown in a herb garden, though the size of the gathered bulbs depends on the amount of sun and moisture during growth. In the early autumn garlic bulbs are lifted and dried like onions.

Marjoram
This spicy aromatic herb is used principally for stuffings, especially for lamb. Though classed as a half-hardy annual, it will grow for 2-3 years without dying off, and will seed itself under normal conditions. When dried it mixes well with thyme and savory for use when recipes call for mixed herbs.

Mints
Many people are unaware that there are several varieties of this perennial herb. The mint that is sold in the shops and grown in many gardens for kitchen use is spearmint. After a few years it is apt to revert towards its wild state, ie. get coarse and harsh in flavour. For growing at home the Bowles variety of mint (Mentha rotundifolia) is very satisfactory. It has large rather woolly leaves and is excellent for a mint sauce and general flavouring.

Other mints are the scented ones : apple, pineapple and eau-de-cologne, the two latter being especially good in a fruit or wine cup and for use as a tea. Apple mint is a good substitute for sage in a savoury stuffing and for flavouring an apple jelly.

Parsley
The most usual and common herb of all is parsley, called in earlier days the herb of health. Nowadays it has been relegated to a garnish, which is a pity as it can be made into a good jelly (to eat on bread and butter) or a delicious soup. It is one of the three ingredients of a bouquet garni. Use the stalks for this as they have the most flavour, and use the leaves for chopping. Freshly chopped, but not too finely, and sprinkled thickly over such dishes as egg mayonnaise and fish cooked in various ways, it gives a wonderful flavour. Fried with fish, it is delicious and there never seems to be enough of it !

Parsley takes a long time to grow and is slow in germinating, so for those who are impatient, it is wise to buy parsley plants in the spring from a nurseryman. Parsley is not worth drying as it can be bought (or picked from the garden) all the year round. Though a biennial, parsley is best treated as an annual and fresh plants put in every year.

Hamburg parsley
Like parsley, this biennial can be treated as an annual. The plant has large sprays of leaves similar to a carrot though not so feathery, and the root is white like a small carrot.

Both leaves and root are used, the former chopped in stuffings and soups, notably bortsch, and the root for grating to flavour ragoûts and salads or in a bouquet garni. It can also be eaten as a vegetable, but in this case the plants must be thinned out when half grown, like carrots.

The flavour of both leaves and root is delicate, tasting (as its name suggests) like parsley.

The roots are lifted in the ▶ 109

Herbs continued

autumn, like root vegetables, and may be stored.

The value of Hamburg parsley is its availability for flavouring during the winter months when ordinary parsley is scarce.

Rosemary
A bush rather than a plant, this perennial herb is not always associated with use in the kitchen. Indeed, being strong and pungent, it should be used in the spray, or a few of the needle-like leaves can be stripped from the stem and used whole. A few cooked whole with sauté potatoes give a delicious flavour. Put a spray in the roasting tin when cooking chicken or lamb in the oven.

Sage
This perennial herb is the one most associated with goose, duck or rich meats. It is strong in flavour, so 3-4 leaves are usually enough for a stuffing. It can also be used to flavour crab-apple or gooseberry jelly.

Savory
A useful herb that has an aromatic flavour similar to marjoram. It has a dark green, pointed leaf and it is especially suited for flavouring broad beans.

There are two varieties, the

1a *Bayleaves (fresh)* **1b** *Bayleaves (dried)* **2** *Chives* **3** *Dill* **4** *Fennel* **5** *Garlic* **6** *Marjoram* **7a** *Mint (Bowles)* **7b** *Mint (scented)* **8** *Parsley* **9** *Rosemary* **10** *Sage* **11** *Savory* **12** *Tarragon* **13a** *Thyme* **13b** *Thyme (lemon)* **14** *Balm* **15** *Basil (sweet)* **16** *Florence fennel* **17** *Hamburg parsley* **18** *Poppy*

Herbs continued

annual summer savory, and perennial winter savory, the latter being more usually home-grown.

Tarragon
This is a perennial which is best home grown as it is not easily obtainable in shops. When buying plants make sure to get the right kind, which is the French variety, with its faint flavour of aniseed and a grey-green, slightly pointed leaf when full grown. 'Russian' tarragon is frequently mistaken for this variety but it is green and rank in comparison and has no scent at all.

This herb, which goes particularly well with chicken, fish and eggs, is delicate in flavour. It also makes an aromatic vinegar for use in salads and sauces.

Thyme
This is a perennial herb; the most commonly used varieties are the black and lemon thyme. The former is distinguished by its narrow leaf, the latter by a broader and brighter green leaf and a strong lemon smell.

Thyme is also used in a bouquet garni and chopped in all savoury stuffings. It dries well.

Spices

Caraway
Like coriander this biennial is grown for the seeds. These are used mostly dried, in cake mixtures and bread doughs.

Cardamoms
These are the fruit of a reed-like plant. There are about eight kinds, of which the best-known ones are the whitish pods which contain little black seeds — only the seeds are used, in curries.

Chilli
This hot spice is the dried pod of a species of *Capsicum* or red pepper.

Cinnamon
A warm, sweet, aromatic spice suitable for adding to sweet foods and drinks. Most cinnamon comes from the bark of *Cinnamomum zeylanicum*, a tree native to the Malabar coast and Ceylon. The bark is curled to form quills or sticks, or ground to a powder. Another type of cinnamon, *Cinnamomum cassia,* comes from the cassia tree and is slightly more bitter.

Cloves
Sweet, aromatic spices, cloves have many uses, either ground or whole, in both savoury and sweet dishes. An onion stuck round with cloves is a classic flavouring for stocks, soups, stews and some sauces. The flowers of the clove-tree, an evergreen native to the Molucca Islands, are picked in bud and dried in the sun.

Coriander
A feathery annual plant, it is grown mostly for the seeds which, when dried, are ground and used

Great baskets of spices set the scene at an Indian market

in curries and spicy dishes. The old fashioned 'comfit' (seeds coated with sugar) was made with coriander seeds. They are also used for pot-pourri, as their fragrance increases on keeping. The aromatic green leaves may be added to salads and fresh chutney.

Cumin

The five-sided seeds of this plant are long and spindle-shaped, black, dull yellow or light brown in colour, smooth or covered in hairs.

Curry

A generic term for a blend of many spices such as **ginger, chilli, coriander, cinnamon, fenugreek, turmeric, mustard, pepper,** and **cloves.** The blend varies in strength and proportion, the strength being dependent on the amount of **chilli.** Many people, especially in India and the Far East, prefer to grind and mix individual spices to make their own curry, according to the type of food being cooked. However, curry powder can be used for convenience in an ordinary meat or fish dish, or a sauce.

Fenugreek

This herb has slightly bitter, aromatic seeds, used for curry.

Garam masala

This name means mixed spice (masala being Hindustani for spice). It consists of cinnamon, cloves, cardamoms, black cumin seeds, nutmeg and mace. It is possible to buy ready-made garam masala from an Indian

113

Spices continned

grocer, although it is most fragrant if made at home.

Ginger
The rootstock of a ginger plant which has a beautifully scented lily, it is mainly grown in Africa, India, China. It is a hot, sweet and clean-flavoured spice which can be bought in fresh root, or ground form. Both kinds can be used in curries, although the fresh green is better. Green ginger is available only at certain times of the year. It has a thin skin which can be removed if wished. A piece of ginger is peeled off, sliced, then either finely chopped or pounded to a paste. The root may also be either preserved in syrup or dried, or as a crystallised sweet variety used in confectionery. The ground form is best used for cakes, biscuits and sauces, and also in marinades.

Mace
These are the tendrils which cover a nutmeg. When left whole they are termed blade mace, but they can also be ground.

Mustard
This is native to Europe, Asia and North America. The young leaves may be added to a salad, the seeds can be added to curries and used in pickling and vinegars. They may also be crushed and mixed with water, to be used as a condiment.

Nutmeg
This is the seed that comes from the same fruit as mace. Obtainable whole or ground, it is used to flavour milk puddings and drinks, cakes and biscuits.

Poppy
The seeds used in cooking are slate blue and from a different variety than that used for opium. They may be used to sprinkle over bread rolls, or ground and used in cakes, or to thicken curry.

Saffron
This comes from the stamen of the saffron crocus, and gives a yellow colouring. Use it to colour and flavour rice and curry dishes.

Tamarind
The pod of the tamarind tree is used with a little sugar to give a sweet-acid effect. A piece about the size of an egg is added to $\frac{1}{2}$ teacup of boiling water, left to infuse for 10 minutes, then squeezed through muslin. The resulting liquid is then used in a curry. For a thicker infusion use less water. If you cannot get any tamarind, substitute 1 tablespoon redcurrant jelly mixed with 1 tablespoon lemon or lime juice.

Turmeric
An aromatic pungent root of a plant, used ground to colour and flavour curry. Care must be taken not to let turmeric juice stain napkins, as — being a dye — it is hard to remove.

Mixed spice
Usually consists of **coriander, cinnamon, cloves, ginger, nutmeg** and **allspice,** sifted together in varying proportions. Use chiefly for cakes and sauces.

Stuffings

Stuffings.are another delicious way of ringing the changes with traditional fare. Whether you simply fill the cavities in a bird, or whether you bone out the meat and carefully reshape it round the stuffing, you have a simple way of adding both flavour and bulk to a meal. Choose a plain herb stuffing or a rich, meaty forcemeat, to suit your mood ; but don't always stick to your favourites — there are pleasures galore ahead for those willing to try a new idea.

Sage and onion stuffing

3 medium-size onions (finely sliced)
2 oz butter, or suet
6 oz fresh white breadcrumbs
2 teaspoons dried sage
1 teaspoon chopped parsley
salt and pepper
beaten egg, or milk

Method
Slice onions finely and boil for 15-20 minutes in salted water. Drain and stir in the butter or suet. Add remaining ingredients, season well and mix with beaten egg or milk. If the joint is not suitable for stuffing, put the mixture into a small oven-proof dish, baste with 1 tablespoon of dripping and cook in the oven for 30-40 minutes at 400°F or Mark 6.

Liver and kidney stuffing

1 medium-size onion (finely chopped)
2 oz butter
liver and kidneys of 1 pig (minced, or finely diced)
8 oz fresh white breadcrumbs
2 tablespoons chopped marjoram
2 tablespoons chopped parsley
salt and pepper
1 egg (beaten)

Method
Soften the onion in the butter, then add the prepared liver and kidneys ; sauté over brisk heat for 2-3 minutes, then turn into a bowl and cool. Add crumbs and herbs. Season well and stir in the beaten egg.

Ham, parsley and thyme stuffing

2-3 shallots (finely chopped)
2 oz butter
8 oz cooked ham (minced)
1 teacup fresh white breadcrumbs
1 dessertspoon fresh chopped, or dried, thyme and parsley
salt and pepper
1 egg (lightly beaten)

Method
Chop shallots finely and cook in butter until soft. Then add to the ham with breadcrumbs and herbs. Season and bind with beaten egg. Put into the chicken, sew up or secure with poultry pins / lacers and truss into shape.

Ham and veal stuffing

1 oz butter
1 shallot (finely chopped)
6 oz ham (minced)
6 oz veal (minced)
2-3 tablespoons fresh white breadcrumbs
1 dessertspoon chopped mixed herbs and parsley
1 egg (lightly beaten)

Method
Melt butter in a saucepan, add chopped shallot, cook until soft and leave to cool. Mix the minced ham with the minced veal, breadcrumbs, herbs and parsley. Add shallot, season and bind with beaten egg.

Note : the two recipes above are particularly suitable for poussins which have been boned out.

Stuffing alsacienne

½ lb salt belly pork
bouquet garni
1 oz butter
1 medium-size onion (finely
   chopped)
5 oz long grain rice
¾-1 pint stock (made from giblets)
½ bayleaf

Method

First cook the salt port with the bouquet garni in enough water to cover, for 1 hour. Allow to cool a little in the liquid, then remove skin and bones and chop finely.

Melt the butter in a flame-proof casserole, add the onion and rice and cook slowly for a few minutes until the rice looks clear. Then add ¾ pint stock and bring to the boil. Stir the pre-pared pork into the rice with a fork. Add the bayleaf, cover casserole tightly and cook in the oven for about 20 minutes. Test to see if the rice is done and add extra stock if necessary.

For chicken farci alsacienne, take a freshly roasted chicken, cut the suprêmes from each side of the breast and cut away the breastbone. Fill the body with stuffing alsacienne, slice the suprêmes and replace them on the bird

Pork or veal forcemeat

1½ lb sausage meat, or half sausage
    meat and minced pork, or veal
1½ oz butter
1 large onion (finely chopped)
1 dessertspoon each dried mixed
    herbs and parsley (chopped), or
    fresh thyme, sage and parsley
    (chopped)
1 teacup fresh white breadcrumbs
1 egg (lightly beaten)
stock (to moisten)
salt and pepper

Method

Put meat into a bowl. Melt
butter in a pan, add onion,
cover and cook until soft. Add
to meat with herbs, parsley and
crumbs. Mix thoroughly with
egg and moisten with as much
stock as needed. Add 2 good
pinches of salt and 1 of pepper.
(Keep forcemeat in refrigerator
if not using immediately.)

Oyster stuffing

2 cans (6 oz each) of oysters
1 large onion (finely chopped)
6 oz butter
3 cups fresh white breadcrumbs
3 sticks of celery (chopped)
1 teaspoon mixed dried herbs
1 tablespoon chopped parsley
little milk, or water (to bind)

Method

Cook the onion in butter until it
is golden-coloured, add about
one-third of the breadcrumbs
and stir over heat until all the
butter is absorbed. Tip mixture
into a bowl, add the remaining
crumbs, celery, herbs and
seasoning. Drain the oysters,
rinse and drain again ; lightly
chop them, add to the mixture
and bind with a little milk or
water.

*Mixing together the onion, bread-
crumbs and celery for the stuffing,
before adding the chopped oysters.*

*The neck end of the turkey is
stuffed and sewn up and remaining
stuffing is put into body cavity*

Celery, apricot and walnut stuffing

1 small head of celery (thinly sliced)
2 oz dried apricots (soaked overnight)
4 oz walnuts (chopped)
1½ oz butter
2 onions (chopped)
1½ teacups fresh white breadcrumbs
1 tablespoon chopped parsley
salt and pepper

Method

Drain apricots and cut each half into 3-4 pieces.

Melt butter in a pan, add onions, cover and cook until soft. Then add celery, apricots and walnuts. Cook for about 4 minutes over brisk heat, stirring continuously, then turn into a bowl. When cool, add crumbs and parsley. Season to taste.

Sage, onion and pickled walnuts

handful of fresh sage leaves, or
  1 tablespoon dried sage
$\frac{1}{2}$ lb onions (finely chopped)
3-4 tablespoons boiling water
2 cups of fresh white breadcrumbs
1 oz butter (melted)
1 large cooking apple (peeled,
  cored and diced)
grated rind and juice of $\frac{1}{2}$ lemon
1 egg (lightly beaten)
4 pickled walnuts (quartered)
salt and pepper
stock (to moisten)

Method

Put onions in a pan, cover with cold water and cook until tender (about 15 minutes). Drain, turn into a bowl. Pour boiling water on sage. Leave to stand for 5 minutes, then drain. Chop fresh leaves, if used.

Add sage to onions, with crumbs, butter, apple, lemon rind and juice. Bind with egg, add walnuts and season well. Add a dessertspoon of stock if the mixture is too dry.

Pork and liver stuffing

2 lb minced pork, or beef
$\frac{1}{2}$ lb gammon rasher (minced)
liver of goose (minced)
1 tablespoon fresh chopped herbs,
  or 1 dessertspoon dried herbs
few drops of Tabasco sauce
1 teaspoon salt
1 teaspoon ground black pepper
1 teaspoon paprika pepper
1 teaspoon anchovy essence
2 oz fresh white breadcrumbs
2-3 tablespoons sherry, or 1 egg
  (beaten)

Method

Mix the ingredients for the stuffing together ; season well and moisten with sherry (or beaten egg).

Sausage, ham and mushroom stuffing

$1\frac{1}{2}$ lb pork sausage meat
8 oz cooked ham (minced)
2 goose livers (minced)
3 shallots (finely chopped)
6 oz flat mushrooms (washed,
  lightly squeezed and chopped)
4 oz fresh white breadcrumbs
1 tablespoon fresh chopped sage,
  or 1 teaspoon dried sage
pinch of allspice (ground from mill)
pepper (ground from mill)
1-2 beaten eggs (to bind)

Method

Mix the sausage meat, ham, minced livers, shallot, mushrooms, crumbs and herbs together. Season well with allspice and pepper and bind with the egg.

Potato and apple stuffing

1 lb potatoes
2 cooking apples
$\frac{1}{2}$ lb onions (finely chopped)
1 dessertspoon chopped fresh or
    dried mixed herbs
1 oz butter (melted)
salt and pepper

Method
Peel potatoes and put in a pan. Cover with cold, salted water and boil until cooked. Meanwhile put onions in a pan, cover with cold water and boil gently until tender (about 15 minutes).

Peel, core and chop the apples and put in a bowl with herbs. Drain the potatoes, mash with a fork, drain onions and add both to apple mixture with the butter. Mix well and season to taste.

Potato stuffing

3 medium-size onions (finely
    chopped)
1$\frac{1}{2}$ lb potatoes
4 oz butter, or double cream
1$\frac{1}{2}$ teaspoons dried sage
salt and pepper

Method
Cover the onions with cold water, cook until tender and drain well. Boil the potatoes, drain and dry thoroughly over gentle heat and mash with a fork ; work in the butter (or cream), onions and sage and season well.

Walnut and herb stuffing

1 oz butter
1 medium-size onion (chopped)
4 oz walnut kernels, or cashew
    nuts (chopped)
4 oz fresh white breadcrumbs
grated rind of 1 lemon
1 tablespoon chopped parsley
1 teaspoon chopped sage
1 teaspoon chopped thyme,
    or marjoram
$\frac{1}{2}$ teaspoon cinnamon
salt and pepper
1 egg (beaten)
juice of $\frac{1}{2}$ lemon

Method
Melt half the butter, add the onion and cook slowly until soft but not coloured, drop the remaining butter into the pan and, when melted, add the nuts and fry until golden-brown. Turn the nuts and onions into a bowl, add the rest of the ingredients and mix well.

Adding breadcrumbs to onions and nuts for stuffing for duck

Liver and mushroom stuffing

liver from the duck
2 chicken livers
1 shallot (chopped)
1 tablespoon chopped parsley
3 tablespoons chopped cooked mushrooms
2 tablespoons finely chopped cooked bacon
1 cup fresh white breadcrumbs
1 egg (beaten)

Method
Dice livers and mix with rest of the dry ingredients. Season well and bind with egg.

Pork and ham stuffing

1 oz butter
1 onion (finely chopped)
12 oz pork, or veal (minced)
1 cup fresh white breadcrumbs
1 dessertspoon parsley (chopped)
1 teaspoon dried sage
1 glass dry sherry
3 oz ham (shredded)
8 pistachio nuts (blanched and shredded)
1 egg (beaten)
salt and pepper

Method
Melt the butter in a pan, add the onion and cook until soft but not coloured. Add to the minced meat and breadcrumbs and mix well with herbs, sherry, ham and pistachios. Bind with the beaten egg and season.

Gammon and anchovy stuffing

4 anchovy fillets
3 tablespoons milk (for soaking anchovy)
8 oz cooked gammon (sliced)
1 shallot (finely chopped)
1 teaspoon chopped parsley
pinch of chopped thyme, or marjoram

Method
Soak the anchovies in a little milk to remove excess salt. Lay the gammon slices overlapping on a board, drain the anchovy fillets and place on top. Sprinkle well with the shallot and herbs and roll up to form a tube. Push this into boned lamb and tie up securely.

1 *Place anchovy fillets on gammon slices, sprinkle with chopped shallot and herbs* **2** *Roll into a tube, open up lamb and stuff in*

Brittany stuffing

2 **tablespoons onion (chopped)**
1 **oz butter**
5 **tablespoons fresh white bread-**
  crumbs
2 **tablespoons chopped mixed**
  herbs
grated rind and little juice of 1
  orange
salt and pepper
seasoned flour
beaten egg
browned breadcrumbs

Method
Cook the onion in the butter until soft but not coloured. Add it to the white crumbs with the herbs, orange rind and seasoning. Bind with the orange juice and a little beaten egg. Spread this over the inside of a boned out loin of lamb, roll up and tie securely with string. Roll in seasoned flour, brush with beaten egg and roll in browned crumbs before roasting.

The stuffed, roast loin of lamb is served with glazed onions and carrots

Duxelles stuffing

$\frac{1}{2}$-$\frac{3}{4}$ lb mushrooms
1 oz butter
2 shallots (finely chopped)
1 tablespoon chopped thyme
1 tablespoon chopped parsley
3 tablespoons fresh white breadcrumbs

Method

Wash mushrooms and chop finely ; melt butter in pan, add shallots and 1 minute later the mushrooms, followed by the herbs. Cook briskly for 5-6 minutes, draw aside from heat before adding crumbs and seasoning.

Ham, pork and veal stuffing

2 oz butter
1 small onion (finely chopped)
4 oz mushrooms (chopped)
2 tablespoons fresh white
   breadcrumbs
3 oz cooked ham (minced)
3 oz raw pork (minced)
3 oz raw veal (minced)
Salt and pepper

Method

Melt the butter in a pan, add onion and cook until soft but not coloured, then add chopped mushrooms and cook for 3 minutes. Turn the mushroom mixture into a bowl, mix in the crumbs and minced meats, and season.

Normandy stuffing

1 medium-size onion (chopped)
1 oz butter
3 oz fresh white breadcrumbs
$\frac{1}{2}$ lb raw pork (minced)
1 tablespoon chopped parsley
1 teaspoon dried sage
salt and pepper
1 cooking apple
1 egg (beaten)

Method

Cook the onion in the butter until soft but not coloured, add to the breadcrumbs and when cool work in the minced pork, herbs and seasoning. Peel the apple and grate on the coarsest side of the grater ; add to the mixture and bind with a little beaten egg.

Putting the Normandy stuffing into the pocket of boned shoulder of lamb

Walnut and lemon stuffing

4 oz walnut kernels
1 medium-size onion (finely
   chopped)
$1\frac{1}{2}$ oz butter
$\frac{1}{2}$ cup ($1\frac{1}{2}$ oz) fresh white breadcrumbs
1 tablespoon chopped parsley
1 teaspoon marjoram
grated rind and juice of $\frac{1}{2}$ lemon
1 egg (beaten)

Method
Grind the walnuts through a small nut mill or mincer. Cook the onion in the butter until soft and golden, then add with the nuts to the breadcrumbs and herbs. Mix in the lemon rind and juice and add just enough egg to bind. Season well.

Walnuts and onions are mixed with breadcrumbs, herbs, lemon rind and juice, then bound with beaten egg to make walnut and lemon stuffing

Kidney, ham and spinach stuffing

2 lambs kidneys
6 oz cooked ham (shoulder cut)
$\frac{1}{2}$ clove of garlic
2 oz fresh white breadcrumbs
1 large handful of spinach leaves
   (about 5 oz)
1 small egg
salt and pepper

Method
To skin and core kidney slit skin on the rounded side and draw back towards the core, then pull gently to pull out as much of the core as possible before cutting it off. Cut open and remove rest of core; chop kidney with the ham and garlic. Stir in the breadcrumbs, then finely chop the spinach and add with the egg to the mixture. Season well.

Marinades

Marinate your meat, game or fish to add extra flavour and at the same time make it tender and juicy. Soaking the meat in a mixture of wine, oil, vegetables, herbs and spices adds a delicious something to mildly flavoured meats, and the oil helps to soften the fibres. Most marinades are first boiled and then left to get quite cold before pouring over the meat; turn the joint occasionally and see that the vegetables sit on top of the meat to keep it moist. Then strain off the marinade and add it to the liquid used in cooking. With a boiled marinade for beef or lamb, let the meat stand in it for 24 hours, and for game up to 3 days. Use a quick, uncooked marinade for steak or fish and allow it to stand for 2-3 hours before cooking.

Marinade for beef

(for a joint of about 2 lb)

1 large onion
1 large carrot
1 stick of celery (optional)
1 large clove of garlic (peeled)
6-8 peppercorns
2 tablespoons olive oil
bouquet garni
2 wineglasses red wine
(Burgundy or Burgundy-type,
or any robust red wine)

Method
Cut the vegetables into thin slices, bruise the peeled clove of garlic but leave whole (chop garlic if a stronger flavour is liked). Put these into a pan with the other ingredients, cover and bring to the boil. Simmer for 2 minutes, then pour off and leave until cold.

Marinade for game, venison and hare

Ingredients as for beef marinade, plus :
2 tablespoons red wine vinegar
2 parings of lemon rind
6 allspice, or juniper, berries
(crushed)

Method
Prepare as for beef marinade. Rich, dark meat such as venison calls for extra sharpness and seasoning, and spices can be altered to taste (see braised venison page 131).

Quick marinade

(for grilled steaks, fish, and meat for a terrine)

1 dessertspoon onion (finely chopped, or sliced)
2-3 tablespoons olive oil
1 teaspoon lemon juice, or wine vinegar
black pepper (ground from mill)
2-3 tablespoons Madeira, or golden sherry (for steak marinade)

Method
Lay meat or fish on a dish and sprinkle over the ingredients. Give a good grinding of black pepper to finish. Leave at least 2 hours before cooking.

Braised beef with red wine

2 -3 lb joint topside, or aitchbone,
   of beef
marinade for beef

To braise
1 onion
1 carrot
2 tablespoons oil, or dripping
bouquet garni
1 clove of garlic
salt and pepper
1 wineglass Burgundy
1 wineglass good stock

For sauce
1 tablespoon oil
1 tablespoon plain flour
$\frac{1}{2}$ pint stock
1 teaspoon tomato purée
6 oz button mushrooms

For garnish
8 oz button onions
$\frac{1}{2}$ oz butter
1 teaspoon sugar

Method

Prepare the marinade and leave meat standing in it in a cool place for 24 hours.

Set oven at 325°F or Mark 3. Take the meat from the marinade and dab it dry with absorbent paper. Slice the onion and carrot. Heat a deep braising pan, put in the dripping or oil and brown the meat all over. Take out meat and add the vegetables, lower heat and fry gently until coloured. Put back the meat, add the bouquet garni, garlic (whole or crushed with salt) and seasoning. Pour in the wine and stock. Cover the pan and braise gently in pre-set oven for about 2-$2\frac{1}{2}$ hours or until tender.

Meanwhile prepare the sauce. Heat oil, stir in flour and brown slowly and well. Draw pan aside, add the stock and tomato purée, and strain in the marinade. Bring to the boil and simmer for 15-20 minutes, skim the surface of the sauce occasionally with a tablespoon to remove fat.

Wash mushrooms, trim the stalks level with the caps but do not peel. Add mushrooms to sauce and continue to simmer for 3-4 minutes.

To prepare garnish : peel the onions, blanch and put in a pan with butter and sugar. Cover tightly and cook gently, shaking pan occasionally. In 6-7 minutes the onions will be tender, brown and sticky (ie. glazed).

Remove cooked beef from pan, slice as much as required and keep hot. Boil gravy to reduce a little and strain into the sauce. Spoon enough over the beef to moisten it nicely and serve the rest separately. Garnish the dish with the glazed onions. Serve remaining meat cold next day.

Watchpoint To peel small onions easily, drop into boiling water for 1-2 minutes, then plunge into cold water and drain. Trim the minimum of root and top as too much taken off will make onions fall to pieces.

Braised venison

3 lb venison (taken from the
  haunch)
marinade for venison
pared rinds of 1 orange and
  1 lemon

To braise
dripping (for browning)
2 onions (diced)
2 carrots (diced)
2 sticks of celery (diced)
bouquet garni
½ pint good stock
salt and pepper
1 tablespoon redcurrant jelly
kneaded butter (to thicken)
2-3 tablespoons double cream
  (optional)

Method
Wipe the meat, put into a deep
dish and pour over the cold
marinade ; add rinds. Put prepared vegetables on top and
cover with a lid. Leave 2-3 days
in a cool place, turning venison
occasionally.

When ready to cook, take
meat out of marinade, wipe it
with a cloth, then brown all over
in a pan in the hot dripping.
Remove and put in the diced
vegetables. Cover and cook
gently for 7 minutes, then add
the venison with bouquet garni,
the strained marinade and the
stock.

Season, bring to boil, cover
meat with a piece of greaseproof paper or foil, then the lid,
and braise gently for 2-3 hours
or until very tender in oven at
325°F or Mark 3.

Strain off the gravy, skim well
to remove fat, add the redcurrant jelly and thicken with
the kneaded butter. Reduce by
boiling, if necessary, until sauce
is the consistency of thin cream.
Taste for seasoning. Slice the
cooked venison, put in serving
dish and spoon over the sauce.

For a special occasion add
2-3 tablespoons cream to the
sauce just before serving.

Jugged hare (Civet de lièvre)

1 good hare (with the blood)
1½ oz butter
4 oz rasher of streaky bacon (cut
    into lardons and blanched)
24 pickling onions (blanched)
1 oz flour
1 pint red wine
1 pint stock
4 oz button mushrooms

For marinade
4 tablespoons olive oil
2-3 tablespoons brandy
1 large onion (cut into rings)
3 shallots
3 sprigs of parsley (with the
    root on if possible)
½ bayleaf
sprig of thyme

To garnish
triangular croûtes of fried
    bread

Method

Cut the hare, detaching the legs and dividing the back into 3 or 4 pieces, and put the pieces in the marinade. Leave in a cool place for 24 hours, turning the hare from time to time. Reserve the blood.

Heat the butter in a large flameproof casserole and brown the lardons of bacon. Remove bacon from the pan and place on a plate. Add pickling onions to the pan ; cook slowly until well coloured and then add to the lardons and set on one side.

Add the flour to the fat in the pan and cook slowly until golden-brown. Meanwhile, remove the pieces of hare from the marinade and add them to the pan ; cook with the roux until nicely coloured on all sides (about 10 minutes). Add the wine and stock, stir well and bring to the boil. Cover with a round of buttered paper and a tightly fitting lid ; put in a very moderate oven, pre-set at 325°F or Mark 3, for about 1½ hours.

Take up the hare and strain the sauce ; wipe out the casserole, replace the hare and add the mushrooms and prepared bacon and onions. Pour the strained sauce over the hare and return casserole to the oven for 15-20 minutes.

Just before serving, thicken the sauce with the blood and surround with the croûtons.

Appendix

Notes and basic recipes

Almonds

Buy them with their skins on. This way they retain their oil better. Blanching to remove the skins gives extra juiciness.

To blanch : pour boiling water over the shelled nuts, cover the pan and leave until cool. Then the skins can be easily removed (test one with finger and thumb). Drain, rinse in cold water, press skins off with fingers. Rinse, dry thoroughly.

To brown almonds : blanch and bake for 7-8 minutes in a moderate oven at 350°F or Mark 4.

To chop almonds : first blanch, skin, chop and then brown them in the oven, if desired.

To shred almonds : first blanch, skin, split in two and cut each half lengthways in fine pieces. These can then be used as they are or browned quickly in the oven, with or without a sprinkling of caster sugar.

To flake almonds : first blanch, skin, and cut horizontally into flakes with a small sharp knife.

To grind almonds : first blanch, skin, chop and pound into a paste (use a pestle and mortar, or a grinder, or the butt end of a rolling pin). Home-prepared ground almonds taste much better than the ready ground variety.

Aspic jelly

This is a jelly made from good fish, chicken, or meat stock very slightly sharpened with wine and a few drops of wine vinegar. Care must be taken that the stock is well flavoured and seasoned and that it is not too sharp, only pleasantly acidulated.

With certain delicately flavoured foods, such as fish, eggs or prawns, home-made aspic adds to and enhances the flavour. If you need aspic for brushing over sliced meat, use the commercially prepared variety, which is excellent for this —especially if a small quantity of the water is replaced by sherry. Make up according to directions on the packet or can.

Aspic, and most jellies containing wine, will keep for several days in the refrigerator. To do this, pour the liquid aspic into a jug, leave to set, then pour about ½ inch cold water over the top, and refrigerate. Remember to pour water off before melting the aspic for use.

Basic aspic recipe

2½ fl oz sherry
2½ fl oz white wine
2 oz gelatine
1¾ pints cold stock
1 teaspoon wine vinegar
2 egg whites

Method

Add wines to gelatine and set aside. Pour cold stock into scalded pan, add vinegar. Whisk egg whites to a froth, add them to the pan, set over moderate heat and whisk backwards and downwards (the reverse of the usual whisking movement) until the stock is hot. Then add gelatine, which by now will have absorbed the wine, and continue whisking steadily until boiling point is reached.

Stop whisking and allow liquid to rise to the top of the pan ; turn off heat or draw pan aside and leave to settle for about 5 minutes, then bring it again to the boil, draw pan aside once more and leave liquid to settle. At this point the liquid should look clear ; if not, repeat the boiling-up process.

Filter the jelly through a scalded cloth or jelly bag.

The aspic should be allowed to cool before use.

The stock for aspic jelly may be white (chicken or veal), brown (beef) or fish, according to the dish.

Breadcrumbs

Fresh white crumbs : take a large loaf (the best type is a sandwich loaf) at least two days old. Cut off the crust and keep to one side. Break up bread into crumbs either by rubbing through a wire sieve or a Mouli sieve, or by working in an electric blender.

Dried crumbs : make crumbs as above, then spread them on a sheet of paper laid on a baking tin and cover with another sheet of paper to keep off any dust. Leave to dry in a warm temperature — the plate rack, or warming drawer, or the top of the oven, or even the airing cupboard, is ideal. The crumbs may take a day or two to dry thoroughly, and they must be crisp before storing. To make them uniformly fine sift them through a wire bowl strainer.

Browned crumbs : bake the crusts of the loaf in a slow oven until golden-brown, then crush or grind through a mincer. Sift crumbs through a wire bowl strainer to make them uniformly fine. Store all crumbs in a dry, screw-top jar.

Carrots (glazed)
1-2 lb carrots
1 teaspoon caster sugar
1 oz butter
salt
mint (chopped)

Method
Peel carrots and leave whole, or quarter, if small. If very large, cut in thin slices. Put in a pan with water to cover, sugar, butter and a pinch of salt. Cover and cook steadily until tender, then remove lid and cook until all the water has evaporated, when the butter and sugar will form a glaze round the carrots.

Add a little chopped mint just before serving.

Gelatine
As gelatine setting strength varies according to brand, it is essential to follow instructions given on the pack. For instance. Davis gelatine recommend 1 oz to set 2 pints of liquid.

Onions (glazed)
Cover the onions with cold water, add salt and bring to the boil. Tip off the water, add 1-1½ oz butter and a dusting of caster sugar. Cover and cook gently until golden-brown on all sides, and cooked through (about 10 minutes).

Pistachio nuts
To blanch nuts, pour boiling water over and add a pinch of bicarbonate of soda to preserve colour. Cover pan and leave until cool. Then skins can be easily removed with fingers.

Potatoes, creamed
1½ lb potatoes
1-2 oz butter
¼ pint milk
salt and pepper

Method
Cut potatoes in even-size pieces, if very large, and cook in salted water until tender, taking care not to let water boil away from potatoes.

When potatoes are tender, pour off the water and return pan to gentle heat. With the lid half on, continue cooking for 2-3 minutes until the potatoes are dry. Then add butter (according to taste), season and crush potatoes with a potato masher or fork. Press them down firmly to the bottom of the saucepan and pour on ¼ pint boiling milk. Put the lid on the pan and let it stand in a warm place. The potatoes can be kept warm in this way for up to 30 minutes and they will absorb the milk in the meantime.

Then, just before dishing up, beat the potatoes very well with a wooden spoon, or small electric whisk, until they are light and very fluffy.

Rice

Most people have their own favourite method of boiling rice. That recommended by Asians is to cook the rice in a small quantity of boiling water until this is absorbed, when rice is soft. The amount of water varies according to the quality of the rice. This method is good but can present problems. Really the simplest way is to cook the rice (about 2 oz washed rice per person) in plenty of boiling, well-salted water (3 quarts per 8 oz rice) for about 12 minutes. You can add a slice of lemon for flavour. Stir with a fork to prevent rice sticking while boiling, and watch that it does not overcook.

To stop rice cooking, either tip it quickly into a colander and drain, or pour $\frac{1}{2}$ cup cold water into the pan and then drain. Pour over a jug of hot water to wash away the remaining starch, making several holes through the rice with the handle of a wooden spoon to help it drain more quickly.

To reheat : spoon into a buttered ovenproof dish, cover with buttered paper, put in oven at 350°F or Mark 4 for 30 minutes.

Spinach à la crème

1$\frac{1}{2}$ lb spinach
$\frac{1}{2}$ oz butter
5 tablespoons double cream, or
    béchamel sauce
salt and pepper
little grated nutmeg

Method
Wash spinach until completely clean.

Cook in plenty of boiling salted water for about 8-10 minutes. Drain well and press between two plates to remove any excess water. Rub through a wire strainer or Mouli sieve.

Melt butter in a pan until slightly coloured, add spinach and cook for a few minutes until dry. Then add cream or béchamel sauce and heat thoroughly. Season carefully and add a little grated nutmeg.

Tomato pulp

In season, use rather ripe tomatoes; at other times of the year it is better to used canned Italian tomatoes. To make $\frac{1}{2}$ pint of pulp, take $\frac{3}{4}$ lb ripe tomatoes (seeds removed) or a 14 oz can of tomatoes. Put them into a pan with a clove of lightly bruised garlic, a bayleaf, salt, pepper from the mill and a slice of onion. Add a nut of butter, cover and cook slowly to a thick pulp, about 10-15 minutes. When really thick, pass through a strainer. Adjust the seasoning ; add a little sugar if necessary. The pulp should not be sharp.

Tomatoes

To skin tomatoes : place them in a bowl, scald by pouring boiling water over them, count 12, then pour off the hot water and replace it with cold. The skin then comes off easily.

To remove seeds : slice off the top of each tomato and flick out seeds with the handle of a teaspoon, using the bowl of the spoon to detach the core.

Stocks

As every good cook knows, the best casseroles, stews, braises and sauces owe their fine flavour to the original stock. Poor stock can turn a promising dish into a dull and tasteless mixture. If a recipe calls for good stock and you don't have any to hand (nor feel like making some), then change your choice of dish. Trying to compromise can lead to failure in making a special dish.

Stock is easy to make once you know how, and its ingredients are not expensive. Most larders have something — vegetables, carcass bones and so on — which can be turned into a small quantity of stock for a gravy or a simple sauce. If you want more, a few beef bones from the butcher will make enough stock for a week for the average family needs. Bones, on their own, will make a stronger stock than if you use mixed vegetables and bits of meat (mixed stock).

Raw mutton bones and turnips are best left out of stocks unless you are making a Scotch broth ; both have a strong flavour and could well spoil the dish for which the stock is intended.

The liquid in a stockpot should be reduced in quantity (by simmering) by about a quarter, or even more, before the stock is ready for straining.

In an emergency a **bouillon cube** can be used for certain things, but it can never replace home-made stock because it will lack the characteristic jellied quality. Bouillon cubes are salty and there is always the danger of overdoing the seasoning. If you use cubes too often as the basis of your stock, your dishes will not only have a monotonous flavour but the bouillon cube taste will give you away.

Mixed stock

If you want a really clear stock, the only way to make it is to use raw bones. If you are using cooked ones as well, it helps to add these after the stock has come to the boil, although it is better not to mix raw with cooked bones if the stock is to be kept for any length of time.

Any trimmings or leftovers in the way of meat can go into your regular stockpot : chicken carcasses and giblets (but not the liver) ; bacon rinds ; or a ham or bacon bone. This last is often given away and it makes excellent stock for a pea soup.

Add a plateful of cut-up root vegetables, a bouquet garni, 5-6 peppercorns, and pour in enough cold water to cover the ingredients by two-thirds. Salt very lightly, or not at all if there is a bacon bone in the pot. Bring slowly to the boil, skim, half-cover the pan and simmer for 1½-2 hours or longer, depending on the quantity of stock being made. The liquid should reduce by about a third. Strain off and, when the stock is cold, skim well to remove any fat. Throw away the ingredients unless a fair amount of raw bones have been used, in which case more water can be added and a second boiling made.

If the stock is to be kept several days, or if there is a fair proportion of chicken in it, bring to the boil every day. If you are keeping it in the refrigerator, save room by storing, covered, in a jug instead of a bowl. Remember that the stronger the stock, the better it will keep.

Watchpoint Long slow simmering is essential for any meat stock. It should never be allowed to boil hard as this will result in a thick muddy-looking jelly instead of a semi-clear one.

Bone stock, brown

3 lb beef bones (or mixed beef / veal)
2 onions (quartered)
2 carrots (quartered)
1 stick of celery (sliced)
large bouquet garni
6 peppercorns
3-4 quarts water
salt

6-quart capacity saucepan, or small fish kettle

Method

Wipe bones but do not wash unless unavoidable. Put into a very large pan. Set on gentle heat and leave bones to fry gently for 15-20 minutes. Enough fat will come out from the marrow so do not add any to pan unless bones are very dry. After 10 minutes add the vegetables.

When bones and vegetables are just coloured, add herbs, peppercorns and the water, which should come up two-thirds above level of ingredients. Bring slowly to the boil, skimming occasionally, then half cover pan and simmer for 4-5 hours, or until stock tastes strong and good.

Strain off and use bones again for a second boiling. Although this second stock will not be as strong as the first, it is good for soups and gravies. Use the first stock for brown sauces, sautés, casseroles, or where a **jellied stock** is required. For a strong beef broth, add 1 lb shin of beef to the pot halfway through the cooking.

Bone stock, white

This stock forms a basis for cream sauces, white stews, etc. It is made in the same way as brown bone stock, except that bones and vegetables are not browned before the water is added, and veal bones are used. Do not add the vegetables until the bones have come to the boil and fat has been skimmed off.

Chicken stock

This should ideally be made from the giblets (neck, gizzard, heart and feet, if available), but never the liver which imparts a bitter flavour. This is better kept for making pâté, or sautéd and used as a savoury. Dry fry the giblets with an onion, washed but not peeled, and cut in half. To dry fry, use a thick pan with a lid, with barely enough fat to cover the bottom. Allow the pan to get very hot before putting in the giblets and onion, cook on full heat until lightly coloured. Remove pan from heat before covering with 2 pints of cold water. Add a large pinch of salt, a few peppercorns and a bouquet garni (bayleaf, thyme, parsley) and simmer gently for 1-2 hours. Alternatively, make the stock when you cook the chicken by putting the giblets in the roasting tin around the chicken with the onion and herbs, and use the measured quantity of water.

For jellied stock, add raw bones of the chicken.

Fish stock

1½ lb sole bones
1 medium-size onion
½ oz butter
6 white peppercorns
small bouquet garni
juice of ½ lemon
salt
2 pints water

Method

Slice, blanch and refresh the onion. Wash the sole bones well and drain them. Melt the butter in a large pan and put in the prepared onion, sole bones, peppercorns, bouquet garni, lemon juice and salt.

Cover the pan and put over very gentle heat for 10 minutes. Add the water, bring to the boil and skim well. Simmer gently for 20 minutes, then strain through a fine nylon strainer. Leave stock to cool ; when cold, cover and keep in refrigerator until wanted.

Vegetable stock

1 lb carrots
1 lb onions
½ head of celery
½ oz butter
3-4 peppercorns
1 teaspoon tomato purée
2 quarts water
salt

Method

Quarter vegetables, brown lightly in the butter in a large pan. Add peppercorns, tomato purée, water and salt. Bring to boil, cover pan and simmer for 2 hours or until the stock has a good flavour.

Glossary

Bain-marie (au) To cook at temperature just below boiling point in a bain-marie (a saucepan standing in a larger pan of simmering water). May be carried out on top of stove or in oven.

Blanch To whiten meats and remove strong tastes from vegetables by bringing to boil from cold water and draining before further cooking. Green vegetables should be put into boiling water and cooked for up to 1 minute.

Bouquet garni Traditionally a bunch of parsley, thyme, bayleaf, for flavouring stews and sauces. Other herbs can be added. Remove before serving dish.

Butter, kneaded A liaison for thickening. Twice as much butter as flour is worked into a paste on a plate with a fork, and added in small pieces to the cooled mixture off the heat. Butter melts and draws flour into the liquid.

Croûte Small round of bread, lightly toasted or fried, spread or piled up with a savoury mixture, also used as a garnish. Not to be confused with pie or bread crust (also croûte).

Deglaze To heat stock and / or wine together with flavoursome sediments left in roasting / frying pan so that gravy / sauce is formed. (Remove excess fat first.)

Galantine Veal, chicken or duck, boned, stuffed, cooked and coated with aspic for serving cold.

Infuse To steep in liquid (not always boiling) in warm place to draw flavour into the liquid.

Reduce To boil down sauce or any liquid to concentrate flavour and thicken the consistency.

Refresh To pour cold water over previously blanched and drained food. This sets vegetable colours, cleans meat and offal.

Sauté To brown food in butter, or oil and butter. Sometimes cooking is completed in a 'small' sauce — ie. one made on the food in the sauté pan.

Scald 1 To plunge into boiling water for easy peeling. **2** To heat a liquid, eg. milk, to just under boiling point.

Seasoned flour Flour to which salt and pepper have been added.

Slake To mix arrowroot / cornflour with a little cold water before adding to a liquid for thickening.

Index